Busine

Business Morality

Peter Vardy

Marshall Pickering

Marshall Morgan and Scott
Marshall Pickering
34–42 Cleveland Street, London, W1P 5FB, U.K.

First published in 1989 by Marshall Morgan and Scott Publications Ltd
Part of the Marshall Pickering Holdings Group

British Library CIP Data

Vardy, Peter
  Business morality.
  1. Business enterprise. Ethical aspects
  I. Title
  174′.4

  ISBN 0–551–01892–5

Text set in Baskerville by Photoprint, Torquay
Printed in Great Britain by Cox and Wyman, Reading

This book is dedicated to my father

MARK VARDY
(1896–1974)

A Chairman and director within the Unilever and Beecham Groups and Deputy Principal of Ashridge Management College.

A gentle man

Contents

1. LAW, MORALITY AND RECENT TRENDS   1

2. ACCOUNTANTS AND THEIR RULES   9

3. BASIC ASSUMPTIONS   21

4. SOME ETHICAL SCHEMES   28

5. A QUESTION OF PRIORITIES   48

6. THE COMPANY AND THE EMPLOYEE   58

7. THE DIRECTOR AND THE MANAGER   76

8. THE COMPANY AND THE CUSTOMER   97

9. THE COMPANY AND THE SUPPLIER   114

10. THIRD WORLD INVESTMENT
    AND SUPPLIERS   134

11. THE CITY   153

12. THE COMPANY AND THE COMMUNITY   170

13. RELIGION, MORALITY AND BUSINESS   188

QUESTIONS FOR CONSIDERATION   203

INDEX   208

Acknowledgements

My thanks are due to my wife, Anne, George Wilde SJ, Fionn Moore and Sarah Allen who helped by reading the draft manuscript of this book.

The Economist newspaper, that most sane and balanced journal, has been the source for some of the quoted examples.

My colleagues in business over the years, in many different companies, have taught me much about business morality — the cost of it and how easy and tempting it can be to ignore it. The situations they and I faced showed that morality can be a costly luxury — with the price sometimes being paid by employees. Little recognition is given to those who make hard, but apparently right, ethical choices. Perhaps nothing else can be expected.

PETER VARDY

Devon, UK.
St Clair,

Heythrop College,
University of London, UK.

Pentecost to Advent 1988

Chapter One

LAW, MORALITY
AND RECENT TRENDS

The first 'money laundering' service ('laundering' is the process by which 'dirty' money from crime, drugs, prostitution, etc., is 'washed' through several stages to make it 'clean' and untraceable) was provided by Bugsy Siegel who established the first Casino, the Flamingo, in Las Vegas, to launder Mafia money. 'Sure I'm rich,' he would say. 'I got lucky at the Flamingo' — in other words the money he had could be accounted for due to a Casino win and no-one could prove that this was not, in fact, its origin.

International money-laundering now handles some $30 billion per annum — equivalent to the whole of the Gross Domestic Product of Ireland.

The proceeds of the Brinks-Mat gold bullion robbery at Heathrow in 1983 (around 41m dollars) was apparently laundered through a Swiss bank, a subsidiary of the Hongkong and Shanghai Banking Corporation, and a branch of the Bank of Ireland in South London as well as a bank in Lichtenstein.

Police officers in both Britain and America suspect that, in general, uncooperative bank managers are the single biggest impediment to their efforts to stop money laundering.

One of the world's largest bank holding companies, with branches in 72 countries including the US and Britain, was charged on 11th October, 1988, with running a world-wide ring that laundered money from drug trafficking. In a two-year operation against the Bank of Credit and

Commerce International, US customs officials and British and French drug officers penetrated the alleged operation, which involved the Luxembourg holding company and three of its subsidiaries. Eighty-one people, including eight top officers of the bank, were named in an indictment in the US. They were charged with helping to launder more than 32m dollars — some of it profits from Columbia drug traffickers. The bank, in a statement at the time of the indictment, said:

> . . . at no time whatsoever has it knowingly been involved in drug-traffic-related money-laundering.

The word 'knowingly' is important here. One must assume that the bank did not know or have reasonable grounds for suspicion that it was involved in money-laundering. Moral blame cannot then be laid at its door. Knowledge is a pre-requisite for blame in this area. However many people in business choose not to consider ethical issues and the responsibilities that they have to others — not least their own employees, customers, suppliers and shareholders. It is with such questions that this book is concerned.

In the last twenty years there have been radical changes in the relationship between law and morality. Increasingly Western societies are regulated by the rule of law — displacing reliance on a generally accepted moral code. In the United States, lawyers have come to dominate many large corporations as their detailed knowledge is required to determine what is and what is not permissible.

Under America's Bank Secrecy Act of 1970, banks were obliged to report to the Inland Revenue Service any cash deposit of more than $5000 and any American citizen taking more than $5000 in or out of the country must tell the IRS (the amount was raised to $10000 in 1980). In Britain, the obligations of bankers are much less clearly defined, as under the Data Protection Act it is a criminal offence for a bank manager to breach client confidentiality except where drug money is suspected. The most secretive banks of all are not, as many suppose, in Switzerland. Swiss banks will allow police to investigate a foreign-owned account if they are satisfied that the money might be the proceeds of a crime and if the police promise to ignore any evidence of tax evasion that they find. Lichtenstein, however, has no such liberal tendencies.

Bankers tend, increasingly, to rely on the rule of law to decide what they will consider as morally permissible. Money launderers take advantage of the rules and increasingly launder money through international trading companies. Who can tell what a Tunisian steel company charges for steel used by a Korean sub-contractor working for an American prime contractor in Egypt?

Twenty years ago organisations like the Stock Exchange, the professional bodies such as company secretaries, actuaries, bankers and accountants as well as directors and managers were ruled by an unquestioned moral code. As an example the stockbrokers motto was 'My word is my bond' — and they meant this. Stockbrokers were honour-able men (there were few women!) who kept their word — even if keeping their word would be personally costly. The same applied in the professions where moral standards were exceptionally high. There were few rules and certainly no laws governing the way the professions operated, but so high were the ethical codes of the members that they could almost always be trusted and relied upon. There were few cases of members of professions abusing the trust of which they were assumed to be worthy. If they did abuse this trust — and if they were discovered — they were outcasts, rejected by their peers and condemned on all sides.

The professions have introduced more and more rules, regulations and 'ethical guidelines' to govern the conduct of their members. No longer is it considered sufficient to trust to personal moral integrity — rules are now laid down. In

3

the same way, directors have become subject to a tighter legal framework designed to ensure that they behave properly — that, for instance, they do not practice 'insider dealing' in which they make use of privileged information to make profits for themselves or members of their family by buying and selling shares in their companies before the information is announced. Insider dealing has been well publicised in recent years and is a criminal offence. The gaps in the law have gradually been blocked so that, for instance, it is now a criminal offence in Britain to use any inside information even if the person using it did not seek such information, as had to be proved in the past. Such practices no longer raise moral issues — they are simply illegal and can be condemned as such. Moral problems arise where the law is silent.

The workings of the Institutes of Chartered Accountants are good examples of the gradual move over the last twenty years from a general expectation of high moral standards to a requirement to obey rules. Up to the mid 1960s there were few regulations governing the way companies prepared their accounts. The 1948 Companies Act laid down certain minimum disclosure requirements — in other words certain minimum amounts of information had to be disclosed each year in the balance sheet and profit and loss account of every limited company. This information was, however, the bare minimum and how the figures were calculated and the way they were presented was left largely to the discretion of the directors.

Company accounts are important as it is through an examination of the accounts that bankers and creditors decide whether to extend loan or overdraft facilities or to grant credit. It is by looking at the accounts that analysts and investors decide whether to buy or sell shares and that one company determines whether to try to take over another. It is by following the profit or loss trends in the accounts that shareholders determine the performance of the management of the company. Frequently bonuses paid to managers and directors are based directly on the profit figures disclosed in the accounts.

Company auditors, all members of the various Institutes of Chartered or Certified Accountants, used to ensure that not only were the legal rules complied with but, more than this, that the company disclosed what it was fair and reasonable to disclose. The auditors' report confirmed that accounts showed:

A True and Fair view of the state of the Company's affairs and of its Profit or Loss for the period under review.

Management rarely argued with auditors and the auditors ensured that the moral as well as the legal code was adhered to.

In the 1960s, however, things started to change. Management no longer felt bound by the old codes. The codes were unwritten and unclear and what was acceptable and unacceptable was far from obvious. New forms of behaviour crept in — the first of the 'asset strippers' appeared. These were individuals or companies who made a bid for an inefficient company which was not making full use of its assets. The company may have been making modest profits on its manufacturing operations and may have been valued on the basis of these profits. I well remember doing the audit of one of the first of the companies which had its assets stripped. The figures are roughly as follows.

(1) The company had two million shares which were quoted on the Stock Exchange at 40p each, thus valuing the company at £800 000.

(2) Annual profits were about £100 000 — in other words the company's share value was eight times its earnings (i.e. the price earnings ratio was eight).

(3) The company manufactured a traditional product from two factories — one in the Home Counties and one in Yorkshire. The two factories employed 700 people. Both factories were owned by the company.

(4) The book asset value per share of the company (the total value of the company's assets disclosed in its Balance Sheet after deducting its liabilities) was £1 000 000 — equivalent to 50p per share.

(5) A takeover was launched offering shareholders in the company 70p for each of their shares — 30p above the current price. Shareholders, of course, were very pleased — they were being offered a 75 per cent increase in the value of their shares and the directors of the company could offer no hope of increased profits which would justify this price. The company was, therefore, taken over at a price of £1 400 000 (two million shares multipled by 70p).

(6) The new owners first closed one of the factories, dismissing 300 workers. They then sold the factory site for £1 500 000. They concentrated production on the second factory and, six months later, sold the business of the company to a competitor which took over the trade marks, stocks, etc., and moved manufacture into their own factory. The 400 workers in the second factory were laid off and this factory was sold for redevelopment at a price of £1 800 000. The redundancy and closure costs were covered by the profit made on selling the business and trade marks of the company to the competitor.

(7) The new owners had thus sold properties for £3 300 000 and they had only paid £1 400 000 for the company — they therefore made a profit of nearly £2 million in under a year.

The new predators or 'asset-strippers' were willing to pay a price considerably in excess of market value and, when they took over a company, they would close down whole divisions and factories and then sell off the property assets. The properties were often worth much more as development sites than they were as factories. Many people lost their jobs, but the argument was that these jobs had to go because the companies were inefficient.

This practice continues today. When British Aerospace was privatised by the government, little account was taken of the tremendous value (running, potentially, into many hundreds of millions of pounds) of the land owned by the company. The land was around certain airfields but some of these were in prime sites and were ripe for commercial and residential development. When British Aerospace took over the Royal Ordnance factories, they again did so at a price that did not take into account the potential development value of the land. As the Royal Ordnance group is rationalised and factories closed, so British Aerospace is likely to reap substantial property profits from the redevelopment of the sites. When British Rail is privatised, the biggest difficulty may come in putting a realistic value on its land bank — British Rail is one of the largest landowners in Britain.

Obviously all sorts of moral questions arise from these types of situations. Was it 'right' for the asset stripper to act as he did in the example above? Was the previous management of the company 'right' to continue to run the factories as they had been doing when they could have closed them, sold off the sites and reaped the benefits for the shareholders (after all, if in the above example the directors had followed the same course as the asset stripper, the value per share to the shareholders would have been £1.65 instead of the 70p they actually received)? Was the British government 'right' to sell off Aerospace and the Ordnance factories at prices which appeared realistic at the time but which did not take account of the development potential of the land they owned?

It is practical problems such as these that any book on business morality that is going to be relevant to the businessman must address. Academic theory is one thing, the hard facts of the business market-place can be quite another and sometimes academics seem to consider that the business world is as civilised and safe as their own, rather than it being something of a jungle where the rule is 'prosper or die'.

Morality must be seen in positive rather than solely

negative terms. Being moral is not just a matter of not doing certain things or avoiding certain types of behaviour. Good ethical practices should be positive. They should involve individuals and companies being active in the pursuit of the good and not simply negative in avoiding the bad.

In the chapters that follow we shall discuss the moral issues that arise between companies and employees; between directors and managers; between companies and suppliers, customers, shareholders and the community as well as issues relating to the Third World and the conduct of City institutions. The answers to these issues need to be considered by everyone in business as they effect everyone in the day-to-day conduct of their affairs. Ideally, the approach taken to the dilemmas that arise should be philosophically sound and capable of being applied in practice. Answers will not always be given because individual circumstances often alter cases, but hopefully some of the central questions will be raised and readers will be encouraged to think through the issues for themselves and to make up their own minds.

Questions for consideration

At the end of the book, some suggested questions are provided which arise from each chapter. These are intended for use as an aid to personal reflection or to assist in a discussion forum.

Chapter Two

ACCOUNTANTS AND THEIR RULES

Today, managements are greatly concerned to ensure that they meet the legal requirements governing the way their companies' accounts are prepared. Some years ago, when I was working for a large international firm of Chartered Accountants, I well remember being present at a conversation between the chairman of a reasonably large quoted company and the audit partner responsible for his company's audit. This chairman was himself a chartered accountant and knew what he was doing. The audit was nearly over and my staff had produced a list of final queries which had to be taken up with the chairman. The discussion went as follows:

AUDITOR: I am a bit concerned at the way your figures have been presented in your accounts. You have incurred various costs in the year which you have written off directly against your reserves and this gives a somewhat misleading impression to the untrained eye. If these costs had been charged against your profits, there would have been a fall comparing this year with last year. As you have drawn up your accounts, your company's position looks stronger than it might otherwise do and I would like to see an alteration.

CHAIRMAN: That is very interesting. Tell me, do our accounts comply with the Companies Acts and do they meet the regulations of the Accounting Standards Committee?

AUDITOR: Yes, but . . .

CHAIRMAN: Please answer my question. Do these accounts comply with the law or do they not?

AUDITOR: Yes, they do. However I do not think they give a fair picture of what is happening to your business.

CHAIRMAN: I note what you say. If you want to apply your own standards to company accounts may I suggest that you go and get your own company and run it as you wish. This is my company and my accounts. I am willing to discuss with you any inaccuracies in the accounts or any places where we have failed to comply with the law. Apart from that, I think we are wasting my time and yours.

The chairman was right. The auditor had no right to alter the company's accounts. He had two alternatives — to give a clean audit report or to qualify the accounts, and the accounts could only be qualified if the Companies Act or the Statements of Standard Accounting Policy had been infringed. There was, of course, a third option — to resign. But, then, the auditor had his living to earn and no rules were actually being broken. Perhaps he was weak, but he signed.

The emphasis on the value of company assets and performance makes it increasingly important for companies, in order to defend themselves from takeovers and in order to impress bankers, creditors and others, to maximise their profits and to show their property and other assets at the highest possible value in their accounts. In the example in the previous chapter, the company had shown its factory properties in the accounts at their cost value — they were, therefore, grossly under-valued, as the properties had been bought many years previously and prices had increased. Company directors soon learnt that this was foolishness and they carried out frequent revaluations of their assets to ensure that the current values were reflected in their published figures.

This was not just a matter of prudence, it also helped shareholders to judge the companies that they owned more accurately. If the company cited had shown the true value of its assets in the accounts, shareholders would soon have realised that the rate of return on assets employed was simply too low. If, for instance, the factories had been rented rather than owned, the rent payable would have ensured that the company ran at a substantial loss.

It became increasingly crucial for directors to put the best face on things, to try to show as attractive a position as possible to shareholders, bankers, creditors and others. The directors needed to justify their own positions and, they might have said, to protect their employees from the activities of the predators. They wanted to show high profits or to minimise losses, they wanted to show an attractive asset position. They were, of course, still prepared to obey the law, but the legal requirements regarding information to be disclosed to shareholders was set at a very low level indeed. Directors started, therefore, to argue with their auditors and to resist pressure to disclose information unless it was specifically required by law. Rather like many governments in Britain when it comes to security matters, directors felt that the less their shareholders knew the better!

At the end of the 1960s, the professional Institutes of Chartered and Certified Accountants responded to this situation. They set up a body called the Accounting Standards Committee (ASC). The ASC included representatives from Industry, the Civil Service and the accountancy profession. The ASC started to produce, they are still hard at it, a series of guidelines called Statements of Standard Accounting Policy (SSAPs) which set out minimum levels of information that had to be disclosed by every company. Many different areas in the accounts were dealt with and the new rules specified the accounting treatment to be followed or, at the least, narrowed the range of options from which choices could be made.

11

All chartered and certified Accountants who audited company accounts were compelled by their Institutes to ensure that companies abided by the new rules. If companies failed to do so, the auditors were required to qualify the accounts — in other words to declare that the accounts did not comply with recognised accountancy standards. This was a considerable sanction as no director, banker or city investor would tolerate a company that did not keep to the rules.

The new SSAPs, therefore, almost had the force of law because if companies did not comply with them they could not get their accounts audited or, at least, they could not get a 'clean' audit report. Since the ASC was established, more and more rules and regulations have appeared, refining ever more tightly the way accounts are prepared and information is disclosed. There are now more than thirty Statements of Standard Accounting Policy in issue and a number of Exposure Drafts in addition (these are the draft SSAPs which are circulated for comment and discussion before the SSAP itself is finalised). Every year the rules governing the way accounts are prepared become tighter and there is less room for individual initiative by management or auditors.

The government has, however, not been content to leave the accounting bodies to regulate accounts preparation. In the 1981 Companies Act and its subsequent amendments, the government has established on the statute book even more comprehensive disclosure requirements which have the force of law behind them. If Company Law is taken together with the SSAP rules, there is now a huge body of regulations governing the way in which a company prepares its accounts.

There are great advantages in standardised accounting treatments — analysts and investors now know that the many rules are being complied with and this makes it somewhat easier to compare accounts of different companies. There is, however, a tremendous disadvantage. The rules have become so complex that very few people can actually understand what the accounts mean! This is not exaggerated — for ten years, apart from my other business activities, I lectured to managers of Britain's largest clearing bank and for five years I ran training courses in credit appraisal for one of the largest Swiss banks in London. The individuals who went through the training courses certainly came to realise some of the problems of accounts' interpretation — but this hardly went any further. Bank managers are not trained in any detail in the accounting rules and yet they are much more skilled than the average investor.

The accounting rules are so complicated now that many of the trained investors and creditors who rely on these accounts no longer understand what is going on. The rules have expanded to such an extent that the value of the accounts has almost been diminished. This is particularly the case when dealing with multinational groups or in the case of companies which are embarked on an active acquisition policy where comparison of one year with another can be very difficult.

As an accountant, this gave me a great advantage — I could use the accounting rules to disguise from bankers and others what was actually happening in the accounts of companies with which I was involved. Everything would be perfectly legal, but by taking advantage of my knowledge of the sophisticated rules and regulations, by planning company affairs to best advantage, I could ensure that the average banker would gain the wrong impression. Most bankers or analysts have a reasonable knowledge of how company accounts work, but certainly not the detailed knowledge of the ins and outs of the SSAPs that I, as a chartered accountant, have. The accounts would be completely legal, but they might also be misleading to the untrained eye.

The first reaction by many people who are not familiar with this situation is surprise. The second is to believe that this will only happen in a minority of situations or with smaller companies. This is very far from the case. Every company uses some or other form of 'creative accounting' technique to put the best face on things. Many and various are the methods used, but some examples may help to show how widespread the practice has become.

(1) The Chairman of British Coal, Sir Robert Haslam, said when publishing the annual results that presenting the accounts of nationalised industries had become: 'Something of an art form.'

This is, indeed, the case and the interpretation of the figures presented is not so much a science but nearer a craft. British Coal's accounts include a plethora of deficit, social, restructuring and readaptation grants and it is almost impossible to deduce what the 'real' (if there is such a figure) profit or loss was for any given year. The operating loss which was announced was £540 million. This was, however, after taking credit for huge allowances from the government and European Commission for particular purposes and also after paying interest to the government of £368 million on loans made to it of over £4bn. If this interest was excluded, the losses would have been very much reduced. However, the loans covered the massive losses that British Coal has incurred over recent years and it is debatable whether interest should be paid on these. Before British Coal is privatised, all these losses will be written off, thus making the results of the company look much more attractive to private shareholders.

Losses of British Coal increased from £288m to £540m; turnover fell from £4.515m to £4.388m; there was a decline in deep-mine output; overtime increased thus reducing profits and currency movements (which were not covered against) caused further losses. Yet the chairman could claim that this was 'a year of solid achievement'. The word 'achievement' can, of course, cover many situations.

(2) Before British Airways was privatised the chairman

requested that the entire Concorde fleet of aircraft be written down to a NIL VALUE in the accounts. Keith Russell, Chief Accountant of British Airways, wrote to me in November 1988 explaining the position as follows.

Following discussions with HM government, and linked with new arrangements for the financial structure of British Airways in relation to Concorde, the book value of Concorde assets were written down by £135.8m in 1978/9, which effectively reduced the Concorde fleet to NIL book value at 31st March, 1979.

Subsequent capital expenditure on the Concorde fleet was initially depreciated using a basis that would bring this capital expenditure to NIL book value by 30th September, 1986 . . . This capital expenditure was, with the agreement of HM government, subsequently written down to NIL by 31st March, 1983.

The cost of certain specific inventories of Concorde spares acquired from HM government, under the terms of an agreement in March 1984 terminating HM government's involvement in Concorde profits and spares support, was capitalised and written down to NIL over 5 years to 31st March, 1988.

The position, therefore, is clear. By 1979, the hugely expensive Concorde fleet was written down to nil. Then more expenditure was capitalised on the fleet and this was again written down to nil before privatisation.

Concorde, whilst a wonderful technical achievement, was an enormous financial white elephant and the aircraft did not make money if its true cost was taken into account. No airline bought Concorde except for the State carriers of Britain and France — British Airways and Air France.

However, by insisting on the write down of the whole Concorde fleet to nothing, the privatised British Airways was guaranteed to make a profit on Concorde operations — provided that income only had to cover maintenance and operating costs. Once the aircraft were written down to a nil value there was no depreciation at all to be written off. The picture of Lord King, Chairman of British Airways, proudly holding a model of Concorde as he announces the results of his company is mildly amusing, since the whole fleet cost his company nothing and stands in its book at a nil value — a fact that would probably come as a mild surprise to most people. It is not difficult to make a profit if the asset used to make the profit has no cost!

In 1988, British Airways had its fleet of aircraft revalued and thereby increased the value of its fixed assets by £288 million. To quote again from Keith Russell's letter:

> The values of the younger fleets, namely Boeing 737s, most of the Boeing 747-236s and TriStar 200s, were increased by £123m and those of the older fleets namely Boeing 747-136s, TriStar 1/50s and BAC 1-11s were increased by £154m.

When one company takes over another, the opportunity is provided for the assets of the company taken over to be revalued and the life of the assets reassessed. An example will illustrate this.

Assume Airline A takes over Airline B. Airline B has a fleet of Boeing 747s which have been written down in their accounts to £150 million and are considered to have a remaining life of five years. On this basis, an annual charge for depreciation of £30 million will be required. The new owners revalue the aircraft to £240 million. This gives an immediate £90 million increase in the asset value of Airline B and makes the purchase appear much more attractive. The estimated life of the aircraft is now reconsidered and it is decided that the aircraft can continue to operate for ten years. If the £240m value is divided by ten years, a depreciation charge of only £24 million per year is required — this is £6 million less than charged by Airline B prior to the takeover and so future profits coming from this company are immediately increased by this figure — the credit for this increase goes, of course, to the management

of Airline A who are assumed to have 'turned round' the
fortunes of the company being taken over.

(3) When the Birmingham Tyre and Rubber Co. (BTR)
took over Dunlop, the ailing tyre maker, no account was
taken of the massive surplus on the pension fund. Dunlop
had many employees and had agreed to pay pensions at a
certain rate. However the investments in the pension fund
had done so well that the fund held millions of pounds more
than was needed. It was considered that this surplus did
not belong to the employees but to the company. BTR,
therefore, gained control of a huge surplus.

Many companies are now trying to buy other companies
in order to get their hands on their pension-fund surplusses.
These surplusses can be used in different ways, for instance:

(a) they can just be credited back to the profit and loss
account or reserves of the company, thus boosting its
asset value after the takeover,

(b) they can be left in the pension fund, but the
company may take a pension fund 'holiday' so that they
do not have to pay into the pension fund for a number of
years. This reduces their costs and thus increases their
profits — again making the acquired company look a
more attractive buy than it would otherwise have been.

(c) they can be used to increase the pensions payable to
retired employees (this step is rarely taken).

(4) House of Fraser and Debenhams are both department
store groups, yet they have a radically different attitude to
profits and losses on property sales. House of Fraser do not
consider profits on property sales to be part of the normal
operating profits of the group — they are therefore shown
separately as extraordinary items. Debenhams, by contrast,
takes such profits directly to its profit and loss account. In a
time of rapidly rising property values, Debenhams' profit
figures will, therefore, look better than House of Fraser's
even though the trading position of the two may be the
same.

(5) Sainsbury's, when it is developing a new store, capitalises interest paid on the development costs incurred whilst the store is being built rather than writing these costs off against profits. The result is that Sainsbury's results look better than store groups which do not follow this practice.

The advent of new and tighter regulations governing accounts' preparation has had even more severe disadvantages. Twenty years ago there were few legal requirements but a high moral code. Today there are very many legal and quasi-legal requirements, but the idea of a moral sense has largely disappeared.

None of the different accounting treatments set out above are 'wrong' — indeed they can all be readily justified. Where the legal has become the same as the moral, everything is permitted provided the laid-down rules are not broken. The more rules that are laid down however, the more company directors are allowed to do anything that they can think of provided only that the rules are complied with and the more complex accounts become.

Since the dispute between auditor and chairman set out at the beginning of this chapter took place, the 1981 Companies Act has introduced a new requirement enabling auditors to qualify accounts even if all the legal disclosures have been made if, in the opinion of the auditors, the accounts do not fairly present the company's financial position and its profit or loss for the period under review. In a way this is good news but, again, we are back to a subjective opinion as to what is or is not 'True and Fair' and most auditors would be very reluctant to take too strong a line in this area if the company had complied with all the rules and regulations. As in all parts of the business arena, competition between professional firms is increasing all the time and, if one professional firm takes a line contrary to the wishes of the directors, there may be other firms who may be prepared to be more 'reasonable'.

What has happened, therefore, is that the area of morality has been taken over by what is legal. What is morally acceptable has become what is legally acceptable. If the businessman or employee can get away with something in law, then many people no longer consider that any moral issues or moral problems arise. Indeed even the phrase 'get away with something' is questionable — British Airways are not 'getting away with anything' by putting a nil value on their Concorde fleet — the information is available for anyone who wishes to examine the figures. It may just seem slightly odd to the average ignorant layman that all these beautiful aircraft, the only ones in the world capable of flying passengers at nearly twice the speed of sound, are worth nothing in the accounts.

The restriction of the morally acceptable to the legally acceptable is by no means restricted to the accountancy sphere. The legality approach to morality also operates in dealings between employee and employer, between company and creditor or customer, between banker and client, between management and staff or unions — in short it is a problem affecting all aspects of business life.

If what is moral is simply what is legal then this book is irrelevant. All that is then required is for the businessman or woman to obey the law. However my contention is that the sphere of the moral is wider than the sphere of the legal and businessmen and women need to consider what, if anything, their moral obligations are. We cannot abdicate moral responsibility and leave it to governments to determine what is right and wrong. Certainly we must not break the law, but our obligations to others do not stop at keeping the law — our moral obligations are wider and more demanding.

Summary
Increasingly the law regulates all aspects of business life. Whereas unwritten moral codes used to guide the actions of managers and professional men, today ethical codes, guide-

lines and the rule of law seem to be taking over. The danger of this is that what is moral becomes what is legal. The issues facing people in business have become more complex and difficult to resolve than ever in the past. There is a need for each of us to consider where we stand on moral issues that arise in the real world and to determine how we will react to the dilemmas they pose or, alternatively, to abandon any moral sense and simply to do whatever the law will allow us to get away with.

Chapter Three

BASIC ASSUMPTIONS

Before we can determine how business morality should be approached and the framework within which the businessman or women should conduct his or her affairs, we need to go back to some first principles. We need to ask ourselves about morality in general and how it is grounded. What *is* morality?

If someone arrives at a conclusion as a result of rational argument or thought, or if an individual advocates a particular course of action, then either the different stages of the argument can be challenged or the assumptions on which the whole debate rests can be questioned.

Take the basic and well known example:

MAJOR PREMISE: All men are mortal
MINOR PREMISE: Socrates is a man
CONCLUSION: Socrates is mortal.

This is an example of valid reasoning beginning from valid premises. However we can alter the premises:

MAJOR PREMISE: All men are happy
MINOR PREMISE: Socrates is a man
CONCLUSION: Socrates is happy.

This is a valid argument — in other words the structure of the argument is valid. The major premise is, however, false. All men are not happy. We can dispute the conclusion by challenging the assumption on which the argument is based.

All arguments rest on some form of assumption. Philosophers have traditionally sought foundations for knowledge. They have looked for a starting position that is as certain as possible. Just as a house must have secure foundations so, it has been held, some things must be certain if we are to claim to know anything at all. There have been two main possibilities suggested which could act as foundations for knowledge: experience and rationality.

1. Experience

Empiricists believe that we can trust our senses more than anything else. If we can see, touch, hear or feel something, then we can be sure of it. St Thomas was an empiricist when he refused to believe in Jesus' resurrection unless he saw and felt the imprint of the nails and the wound in Jesus' side. He refused to believe second-hand reports and insisted on personal, sense experience.

For the empiricist, our knowledge rests on foundations such as those things that we see clearly and distinctly (John Locke). Our bedrock certainties are grounded in those things that we can experience. It is on this bedrock that all our claims to know rest. If I stand in front of my wife, listen to her voice and perhaps even touch her (just to make quite sure that she is not a hologram), then by experiencing her in this way I achieve ultimate certainty. All my claims to knowledge will, therefore, derive from or depend on some sense experience.

2. Rationality

The rationalist, by contrast, is suspicious of sense experience. He or she may point out that experiences are often deceptive. We are continually misled and have to learn to interpret our experiences — we cannot simply rely on them. If we put a straight stick into water, it appears bent. Mirages have deceived many in the desert when the sun shines on the sand and gives the appearance of water. The sun appears to go round the earth. If there is a motor car accident, the people who saw it often describe the accident in very different ways. Advertising photographers are skilled in presenting products in the most attractive possible light. Much depends on the interpretations we bring to our experience.

If, therefore, we need to be sceptical about our experience, we must look to our minds for certainty. Only by looking within ourselves and trusting our reasoning can we arrive at truth.

The French philosopher, Rene Descartes, did this when he set out to find something that was certain. He began by doubting everything — he refused to trust experience and sought instead something about which doubt would be impossible. He found this within his own mind. Everything outside himself he could doubt — there was, however, one thing of which he could be certain. Given that he was thinking, he could not doubt his own existence. This gave rise to Descartes' famous saying: 'COGITO ERGO SUM', 'I think, therefore I am'. Because he was thinking, he simply could not doubt that he existed. On this foundation (the certainty provided by looking into his own mind), Descartes considered that all knowledge was built.

Both of these alternative ideas of, firstly, experience and, secondly, the contents of our own minds, have been considered to provide the royal route to knowledge. Knowledge is claimed to be based on one or other of these strong foundations and, because they are strong, it has been held that we can be confident about our wider knowledge claims. More recently, however, the whole idea of knowledge having foundations has been challenged. Philosophers such as G.E. Moore ('In defence of common sense') and Wittgenstein ('On Certainty') rejected the very idea of bedrock certainties on which all our knowledge rests.

Imagine a young child asking a familiar series of questions to a more or less patient mother:

CHILD: Why do you want to sit down?
MOTHER: To rest my legs.
CHILD: Why do you want to rest your legs?
MOTHER: Because they get tired when I stand up for a long time.
CHILD: What do we sit down on?
MOTHER: Chairs.
CHILD: Yes, but why is that (pointing to a chair) called a chair?
MOTHER: Because that is just what we call a chair. Go off and play like a good girl!

The naming of an object as a chair is part of our educational process. At our mother's knee we learn to use language — we learn to name things. Our common way of life rests on agreement in judgements. At a very basic level, we simply agree that things are chairs, bookcases or hands. We cannot PROVE that a chair is a chair. It is simply that we learn what tables and chairs are as part of our initial education process. Anyone who seriously doubts that what I am sitting on is a chair cannot have learnt the English language (unless she is a philosopher asking the sort of fundamental questions with which philosophers often occupy themselves and which, whilst fascinating, are of little practical revelance to everyday life).

What has all this got to do with morality? The answer is a great deal. Just as some people hold that knowledge has foundations, so others claim that morality has foundations. Perhaps these foundations rest on the commands of a Church or a Holy book (such as the Bible or Koran); perhaps they rest on rules laid down by an institution or government; perhaps they are based on personal intuitions which cannot be doubted; perhaps they are intellectually based or rest on principles that are considered to be self-evident.

In the Western world, we share a common human frame of reference to our lives. To be sure, education differs between southern Italy and London, between New York and rural Northern Canada but even these differences are disappearing as we become a global society. Television is now in almost every house and programmes are beamed across national barriers by satellite. Increasingly our fundamental values are similar. The assumptions on which our lives rest have a great deal in common. We share a common cultural heritage — a heritage rooted in Greek philosophic thought, in Jewish morality, in Christian insights and in the acceptance that science has much to teach us about the Universe. We share a hatred of bigotry and kant, a dislike of the glib and superficial.

At the most basic level we also share common moral insights. These *are*, however, insights — in a way they are assumptions. They are not foundations which rest on experience or reasoning. They are not foundations that can be proved to be true. They are, nevertheless, the framework of our common world view which it does not make sense (at least to us) to challenge.

Legitimate debate may be possible as to whether or not a country should defend itself with nuclear weapons, whether research on human embryos should be permitted, whether abortion should be legalised, whether it is wrong for a couple to sleep together before they are married or whether genital homosexuality is or is not permissible. However at a more basic level, no discussion or argument is possible.

Someone who cannot see that beating up women for pleasure on Sunday afternoons is wrong, that sexual molestation of children is wicked, that rape is an offence against the basic humanity of the woman involved, that armed robbery is to be condemned or that defrauding very poor old people of their life savings is unacceptable behaviour is simply no longer a part of civilised society. They need to be locked up or, perhaps, given psychiatric help. We cannot enter into a rational debate with these people. What, after all, could we say? If someone sexually molests young children, it just does not make sense to have a cool, calm and collected debate with them as to whether or not this is wrong.

Similarly those who tortured and killed six million Jews in Nazi Germany are simply evil. It makes no difference what reasons or justification may be given for these actions — they are to be condemned. Indeed we must, if necessary, go to war with them to ensure that their activities cease.

If you have a mad dog in your street, you shoot it. We do not shoot people who reject society's most basic moral assumptions, but we certainly do not debate with them. Straightforward rejection is the only course. We cannot compromise. Our morality rests on agreement in judgement on certain fundamental principles which cannot be further justified. We may, of course, differ on the source of these principles. Those with religious convictions may ascribe them to God whilst others may say that they have arisen from us living together in a human society (they may say, for instance, that we have taboos against incest for the very good reason that incest weakens the gene pool or that injunctions against eating pork applied in hot countries where pork decayed very quickly). Some may say that the fundamental moral principles are based on intuition, others may talk of instinct or insight and yet others may claim that the fundamental assumptions can be rationally justified. The important point, however, is that, whatever the source, we accept that our common heritage provides us with some starting assumptions.

This is, at least, a beginning. We now need to try to put some flesh on the first basic principles about which we all agree.

Summary

Our common European cultural heritage leads us all to accept general principles of morality which we cannot rationally justify, but which we also cannot doubt. Various reasons may be given for this common acceptance, but anyone who rejects these principles can be recognised by society as being morally debased.

Chapter Four

SOME ETHICAL SCHEMES

In the film *Wall Street*, the entrepreneur, Gecco, made a fortune and acquired great power and influence. He bought and sold companies and, with them, the livelihoods of thousands of individuals. He relied on 'insider information' — in other words information that was not available to the general investing public and which enabled him to anticipate movements in share prices. When an airline was due to be cleared of blame for a crash, he knew this in advance and knew that the shares would then rise as the way would be open for the airline to expand. He bought heavily and stood to make a great deal of money. On another occasion, by skilful detective work, he learnt that a British entrepreneur was about to launch a large takeover bid. He thereupon bought a large parcel of the company's shares and forced the British entrepreneur to pay him an amount that would give him a high profit on his block of shares which were necessary to secure control.

On some occasions he broke the law, on others he did not. There is nothing legally wrong with using good detective work to find out what a competitor is doing and, once having obtained this information, to use it to make a profit. Whether this is morally acceptable is not so clear.

Gecco had a young assistant who was eventually corrupted by him but 'came good in the end'. This assistant worked for a stockbroker and was under heavy pressure from his firm to generate new business. This pressure, as well as his own greed, contributed to his corruption. His employers' should, therefore, have shared something of the blame, although this was not recognised in the film.

This is not a textbook on ethics, still less is it an academic analysis. Nevertheless if we are to be clear on the principles of business morality, we need to consider the available starting points. In the previous chapter we saw that our common heritage provides a series of framework assumptions which it really does not make sense to doubt and which cannot be realistically challenged. However we need to move from the few incontrovertible examples already cited (effectively 'thou shalt not rape or molest young children', 'thou shalt not beat up old ladies', 'thou shalt not commit armed robbery' and 'thou shalt not defraud poor old people of their life savings') to a more general principle that can be applied to different cases which arise in the business world.

The difficult moral decisions in business *are* difficult and it is not going to help the businessman or woman to cope with these decisions by citing the examples given so far. It is like the ten commandments — they are admirable precepts but it is difficult to get more specific guidelines for day-to-day conduct from them. Some people still try to live by them, but even for these individuals interpretation is required to meet the needs of a changing world.

Many different ethical theories have been suggested over the centuries and it may be helpful to summarise these. The list is far from comprehensive but it will help to set the following discussion in perspective.

1. Old Testament morality

Jews, Muslims and Christians all accept and look to the books of the Old Testament as giving a record of God's dealings with his people. The Jews see, in the stories of Abraham, of Isaac, of Moses and of the Prophets, the story of their role as 'the chosen people'. The Muslims also look to Abraham but they look to God's promise to Abraham's son, Ishmael, and they see themselves as descended from him. Christians, in their turn, see Christ's role as the Messiah foreshadowed in the Old Testament and the incarnation of God as a human being as the fulfilment of the story of Israel.

In terms of morality, the story of God's ten commandments given to Moses are still of great significance today. Generations of children have been brought up on these commandments and their influence is deeply embedded in our culture.

The ten commandments rest on the view that there are set rules as to what is right or wrong, irrespective of the effects these rules may have. This position is to be contrasted with the *consequentialist* who takes into account the consequences or effects that any decision may have.

There can be no question that the ten commandments are excellent rules, although today many do not believe in God. Even for those who accept the existence of God and/or who accept the ten commandments, there are real difficulties in interpreting these rules. What, for instance, is meant by 'Thou shalt not steal'? Stealing is contrary to the law and can never be permitted in a straightforward sense, but when moral dilemmas arise in business, these will not be resolved by this commandment. As an example, is 'insider trading' (using information which is available to directors and certain key figures in a company to buy or sell the company's shares and thus to make a profit before the information is generally released) to be regarded as stealing? Similarly, if someone is 'economical with the truth', this need not be regarded as lying — although it may have the same effect.

The asset stripper described in the first chapter is certainly not offending against any of the commandments, nor is the transport contractor who consistently over-loads his lorries. The commandments are, therefore, admirable, but they do not help a great deal in disputes about business morality in the final decade of the twentieth century.

New Testament morality is, however, a different matter and we will return to this later.

2. Ends justify means

Machiavelli has acquired a bad name. His ideas are today generally associated with somewhat devious and sinister methods of action. He was an attractive personality — but this personal appeal does not validate his approach to moral issues. Like Luther in the religious field, Machiavelli challenged the moral status quo.

Throughout the Middle Ages the Church had built up and enforced a system of morality which was never seriously challenged. With the coming of the enlightenment, the most basic assumptions seemed to be no longer certain — everything was in the melting pot and Machiavelli challenged the existing assumptions about morality in a radical way.

In many ways we are today living in a similar sort of period. The old certainties have disappeared and this gives rise to a moral unease. Nothing seems sure. Nowhere has this been clearer than in the case of sexual morality. Within the space of fifty years Western society has moved from relative prudery (at least in public — private vice has always been common and, in Victorian times, almost acceptable provided it was not discovered) to considerable laxity. Today many young couples live together with no feeling that this may be wrong, abortion is generally considered (at least if this is measured in numerical terms over the population as a whole) to be acceptable in certain circumstances and homosexuality is becoming socially tolerated. It is a far cry from the trial of Oscar Wilde!

The passage from old certainties to new ideas is a difficult one. In business morality as in sexual morality it is easy to move from rejection of the old norms to a feeling that 'everything is permitted'. It was this feeling to which Machiavelli gave expression in his own age.

Machiavelli believed that the means justify the ends and the ends towards which humans should work were clear and straightforward. The objective of human endeavour was to obtain and then to hold political power; to maintain order and to foster general prosperity. Unless the leaders can maintain order and prosperity, then their political power will be threatened. Machiavelli did not think that the general good should be sought for itself alone, but only as a means to the wider end of the maintenance of power.

Moral rules, Machiavelli considered, are obtained by determining the best means to the above ends. It follows that whatever means are required for the maintenance of power may be employed and if a number of groups are all trying to maintain power, then any sense of morality as European culture has traditionally recognised it will disappear. Machiavelli would see no difficulty in breaking promises, in lying, stealing or, ultimately, in committing murder if this was in our own interests. He had a low opinion of human nature, considering that all men were wicked. Based on this assumption, it does not seem so unreasonable to break agreements, as the people with whom the agreements have been made, being themselves wicked, are likely to break the agreements if this is in their best interests.

Machiavelli was a consequentialist — he judged actions in terms of their consequences, not in terms of their being good or bad actions in their own right. Society, for Machiavelli, was unimportant — it is no more than the arena for individual action and the individual owes no moral duties or obligations to other individuals within this arena.

There are some parallels between Machiavelli and the Greek philosopher, Plato. Increasingly (and we can recognise this today) political decisions have a considerable effect on the lives of individuals. The moral choices an individual has to make are more and more determined by the law and rulings laid down by politicians. Politics is dynamic — it is continually changing society and the outlook of individuals.

Plato considered that morality and politics were closely related and considered that the state should be ruled by philosopher/guardians. Only the philosopher was well educated enough to be able to govern a state correctly. Plato, however, thought that morality was not just a matter of means towards some wider end. He considered that just and good actions in some way participate in the perfect heavenly Forms of Justice and of Goodness which are independent of the material world. Plato, therefore, would not have tolerated means that Machiavelli would have accepted.

Machiavelli decided on his ends and, once this decision was made, any action was permissible that furthered these ends. Actions could not be condemned as right or wrong in themselves — everything depended on the ends for which they were undertaken. Some business people operate with a similar system of morality today. They first decide on their end — for instance this might be maximising profits or staying in control of the business — and *any* means that contribute to this end is then justified. On this basis, defrauding old ladies of their life savings or making false statements to shareholders or others would be perfectly acceptable provided this increased the profits of the firm or enabled the directors to retain control.

3. The greatest happiness principle

Utilitarian ethics has as an underlying objective, the 'greatest happiness principle'. It claims that the aim of morality should be to provide the greatest happiness for the greatest number of people. Everyone desires happiness or pleasure and, under this theory, our actions should be guided by the general rule that whatever we do should aim to maximise pleasure — not simply for ourselves but for the greatest number of people. In a way, it should be possible to do a form of mathematical calculation to determine how much happiness particular actions will cause.

Sometimes we may have to put our own pleasures in second place where to do so means that the happiness of others can be increased. At face level, this view has considerable appeal — most of us do, after all, seek to avoid pain and to maximise our pleasure. There are, however, very real difficulties.

Utilitarians start with a jump in their argument which can be challenged. Their first premise is to say:

People seek to maximise their happiness.

This may very well be true. However one cannot move from this to the next step which is essential to the Utilitarian idea:

People should seek to maximise their happiness.

In the history of moral debate, there have always been times when what we are inclined to do and what we should do differ. The Utilitarians try to claim that we should do what we are inclined to do and, if they are going to maintain this position, they need to justify the step. If they do not do so, many will reject their argument almost before is has begun.

It is far from clear what 'pleasure' means. It is a vague, all-embracing word that can cover a multitude of activities. One person may get pleasure from gardening, another from sun-bathing, another from work or seeking power or money, another from helping others. Sadists get pleasure from inflicting pain, masochists from having pain inflicted on them. Many people have hobbies and they find their pleasure in these, others seek their pleasure at the end of a bottle — their pleasure comes from earning enough money to have a really major drinking spree.

Sometimes the pleasures of one group may conflict with

those of another. Might the pleasure that some in Nazi Germany had from the extermination of the Jews outweigh the adverse affects on the Jews? Since there were many more Germans than Jews the possibility is at least open on the basic Utilitarian theory although its very offensiveness exposes the falseness of the position.

It is not at all easy to measure pleasure. At a basic level, one can only talk of pleasures of any kind once one's basic physical needs are met. If we are hungry, thirsty, cold, ill or, perhaps, lonely then pleasure is impossible. On the other hand, if one is thirsty, then a long glass of cool water is a very real pleasure. Pleasures are sometimes increased by abstinence.

I remember one occasion when my family and I travelled through south eastern Europe for several months. I had to fly home on business during the trip, and returned after four days with a bag of chocolate biscuits and other English 'goodies'. My children clustered around and pronounced that they had never tasted a finer chocolate biscuit than those I had brought. Their pleasure was increased because they had not had such biscuits for a considerable time. Back in England, however, such things are routine and, after a time, they cease to give real pleasure — they are taken for granted. Many pleasures are like this, we become satiated and need greater stimuli to continue to regard what was previously a pleasure as being enjoyable. This happens in the case of drugs and sometimes alcohol as well — greater and greater quantities are needed to produce the same effect.

There are other problems with the Utilitarian ideal as well. How does one balance not only conflicting pleasures but also conflicts between the needs of one group and the pleasures of another? Do needs (such as warmth, food, clothing, etc.) always take priority over pleasures? On the face of it, this seems reasonable. Surely, it might be held, people's basic needs must first be catered for before anyone can talk of pleasures? However the issue is not that simple.

What are 'basic needs'? In our society today, these 'needs' may be regarded as quite sophisticated and may extend considerably beyond the basic necessities of life. The 'needs' may be regarded as including a television, perhaps a video, a telephone, a refrigerator and perhaps even an annual holiday. One person's need may be another person's luxury or pleasure.

Certainly if we compare the poverty of the Third World with the affluence of the West, the 'needs' of people in the United States and Britain would be considered as luxury pleasures in many other countries. A great deal is going to depend on personal opinion and these opinions may vary widely.

The Utilitarian ideal is attractive, but it suffers from real difficulties. It is rarely going to give an accurate guide for moral action. It is helpful, nevertheless, in identifying the importance of pleasure and in raising the tension between needs and pleasures. It will not, however, suffice as a basis for business morality.

4. Intuition

Both Machiavelli and the Utilitarians sought guidelines for moral actions based on particular ends. They thought, in their different ways, that the final purpose or end of morality was clear and what was then needed was to consider how these ends were to be achieved.

G.E. Moore rejected this type of position when, in 1903, he answered the question, 'What actions ought an individual to perform?' as follows:

> . . . those actions which will cause more good to exist in the Universe than any possible kind of alternative.

This sounds admirable but, of course, the problem is what is meant by 'good'. Moore refused to be drawn on this — he refused to define 'good' in any terms outside itself. He considered that goodness, like the characteristic of 'yellowness', could not be analysed any further. It was an irreducible concept. Moore maintained that we cannot fail to recognise what is good when we are brought face to face with it.

Moore considered that any definition involved breaking up a concept into a number of separate parts and a definition of good was impossible since goodness has no parts. It is simple and unanalysable. 'Good' may, incidentally, be attractive or pleasant but this *is* incidental — it is not a central part of the meaning of 'good' that it should be either attractive or pleasant. It is quite possible to imagine actions that are good which are neither attractive nor pleasant. This is an important position as if 'goodness' cannot be defined in terms of pleasure, then the Utilitarians are on even weaker ground.

One of the great problems with refusing any definition for 'good', is that it is left to our individual insights or intuitions to 'see' what is good and what is not. Moore uses the parallel with recognising a good friend and he considered that we could simply come to 'see' this characteristic. However, individual intuitions and insights differ and many people mistake 'good friends' for a rather lesser quality. The same could be said for a lack of recognition by many people of what love involves. It always saddens me to see the inscriptions on the inside of many books owned by married couples who have separated. Books they have given to each other are inscribed 'All my love', 'With my love always', 'To the love of my life' or in similar terms, but all too soon this love dies. Presumably the emotion that was being expressed was not the genuine article — the intuition that it was genuine turned out to be false and what appeared to be love had turned into indifference or dislike.

In this century, there have been a number of moral philosophers who have rested their moral beliefs on the primacy of intuition. H.A. Prichard was particularly important in this connection. In an article written in 1912 entitled 'Does moral philosophy rest on a mistake?' he rejected the attempts that had been made to justify morality or to give a reason for it. In particular, he rejected the Christian idea of morality as it involved rewards and punishments after death. Prichard maintained that an individual should do her duty or act correctly for the sake of duty or goodness alone. As soon as any external rewards or sanctions are introduced, the moral worth of the action is undermined.

Imagine that I see one of my students helping an old lady across the street and immediately think 'That is a kind action'. Prichard is maintaining that if the motive for the student's action was either that I should see him and should think better of him because of what he had done or that God should see him and reward his action, then the goodness of his action is debased. On this basis, the atheist who acts morally is in a preferable position to the religious believer as the latter must always ask him or herself whether the motive for the action is as pure as might first be supposed. The atheist, with no belief in God or a life after death, acts morally for no reason outside goodness alone.

The biggest problem with the Intuitionist approach to ethics is that it is so individual. Everyone must consult his or her own conscience and there is no way of sorting out differences between individual intuitions. In the final analysis, there is no way of resolving our moral disagreements as the parties who disagree can each claim the support of their private intuitions. At this point, argument and discussion comes to an end.

A second problem is that there is a logical gap between:

(1) I recognise an action as good, and
(2) I determine to do that action.

Acceptance of (1) does not necessarily lead to acceptance of (2). Intuitions do not explain why I should be motivated to act in the way that they tell me is good. Speaking personally, I may have an intuition that a life of kindness, goodness, gentleness, love and charity is an admirable life, yet this recognition fails to spur me to live this sort of life! I continue to muddle on in a fairly inadequate manner — perhaps recognising ideals but failing to live up to them.

John Dewey modified the basic Intuitionist approach by saying that if we call something good, we are saying that it will give us satisfaction. However, it is not clear whether this satisfaction is the end which is sought — in other words whether we act morally *in order to produce* a feeling of satisfaction — or, alternatively, whether in acting in a way that produces satisfaction, we act morally.

Dewey's ideas led onto an *emotive* theory of ethics: this maintains that when we call something good or bad we are merely expressing our emotions towards an action — we are, as Ayer says, giving a 'persuasive definition'. We attempt to persuade others to act as we wish by calling an action good, and to dissuade others from certain actions by terming these 'bad'. Certainly there is an emotive content to ethics — we rarely call actions 'good' which we are emotionally against. To call an action good or bad does have emotional connotations. However this is far from all that is involved. Morality rests on more than personal judgement.

We have looked briefly at several different ethical schemes. They all suffer from disadvantages and all may give different results if they are applied to the business arena. It is small wonder that there is so much confusion about business morality when there is so little agreement as to what morality in general is all about. If we picked any one of the above schemes, many would object. If, for instance, we decided that the ends justify the means (as Machiavelli or the Utilitarians maintained in their very different ways), then we would have to decide on the end we sought. There would be much disagreement about this and even more disagreement when we came to discuss the means to be used to bring about the end.

If we adopt an Intuitionist or Emotivist approach, a

great deal is going to depend on personal opinion and we do not have a framework within which rational discussion can take place. In the end, on both these bases, we are not in a position to criticise others however bad their behaviour may be.

The position is not as hopeless as it may appear. In the second chapter we saw that our common heritage derived from the ancient Greeks, from Jewish morality, from Christian insights and from the enlightenment (with the place it gave to science), provides a common bond between us, at least at a basic level. No matter what moral theories we may support, we all accept: 'thou shalt not rape or molest young children', 'thou shalt not beat up old ladies', 'thou shalt not commit armed robbery' and 'thou shalt not defraud poor old people of their life savings'.

Perhaps this common acceptance rests on intuition, perhaps we are expressing emotions, but whatever the reason we all accept these views. We have been brought up within a common European heritage (or, if we live in North America, Australia, New Zealand or many other countries which were settled by Europeans we can look back to our European heritage). We have been educated within a society into a particular 'form of life', a particular way of looking at the world. We learned at our mother's knee the importance of compassion, we learned that we should not hurt people unnecessarily, we learned to help weaker members of our society. Most of this learning took place before we went to primary school, but the learning in these earlier years was reinforced as our life progressed. We grew up within a society, sharing a common heritage, and we have come to accept the assumptions of this society.

Some philosophers may say that we are wrong to do this. Perhaps, they may say, there is nothing wrong with sexual molestation of young children or beating up old ladies. If there are such individuals we can safely dismiss them. If that is really their position then, however clever they may be, they are wrong. This does not need proof, we simply know they are wrong. We have seen too many examples in our time of political leaders who did not think individuals mattered — Hitler's concentration camps, Stalin's labour camps and the murderous Pol Pot regime in Cambodia are simply evil. We do not need this to be proved to us nor do we feel inadequate because we cannot prove it in our turn. Whatever the reason, our society had learned the fruits of evil and we can recognise it when we see it.

However, we are still in need of a general ethical theory that can give expression to the common feelings of our society. Possibly the most helpful such theory was put forward by Immanuel Kant and his influence is still with us today.

5. People are ends in themselves

Kant separated two ways of looking at moral obligations or duties. He said there were two types of commands that might direct our action: the hypothetical and categorical imperatives.

(i) Hypothetical imperatives

Hypothetical imperatives are commands based on an 'if'. For instance:

If you want to avoid lung cancer, give up smoking.

If you want to do well in business, work hard.

If you want a happy marriage, remember your wife's birthday.

The command to give up smoking, work hard and remember your wife's birthday are all based on an 'if'. We can simply reject the 'if' and, once this has been done, the command has no more force. If, on this basis, I am not interested in doing well in business or avoiding lung cancer, there is no need for me to work hard or give up smoking. By rejecting the end, I reject the means as well.

Any moral command is hypothetical when it is based on an 'if'. When people say, therefore:

If you want to go to heaven, be virtuous.

If you want people to look up to you, give to charity.

All an opponent will have to do is to reject the premise (in these examples to deny that we believe in a life after death or to say that we do not want people to look up to us) and we then do not have to be virtuous or to give to charity.

(ii) Categorical imperatives

Categorical imperatives are absolute commands, they are not based on any reason. There is no 'if' involved, the commands are absolute. So we might say, 'Do not sexually molest young children'. This is an absolute command or obligation which we all recognise. As soon as we start to give reasons why we should not do this (for instance: 'If you want to avoid going to prison, do not molest young children') we make the categorical or absolute demand into a conditional or hypothetical one. If I am not worried about going to prison, there is no reason why I should not molest young children.

For Kant, moral duties were absolute. We should not be moral for *a reason* — rather morality should be based on *reason*. Hypothetical demands are based on a reason. With these commands, there is always a reason (an 'if') why we should act or refrain from acting in a certain way. Kant did not consider that moral obligations rested on an 'if' — they were absolute.

Reason, however, will show us what is and what is not morally correct. Any rational, reasonable person will be able to see this although once issues become more complex then more careful thought may be required. It is by the use of our reason, not by looking at consequences, that we come to decide whether an action is morally right or not.

Kant avoided laying down absolute moral laws like the ten commandments. He recognised that circumstances alter cases. It is all very well laying down a general rule such as 'Thou shalt not steal', but there are always going to be exceptions. If I find that a friend of mine has purchased poison and intends to use it to kill his girl friend, it is perfectly reasonable for me to steal the poison to prevent him doing this. Any hard and fast rules, therefore, are going to be inadequate in certain circumstances.

It is necessary to establish some general principle for action which can be applied in any situation. Kant had several versions of the Categorical imperative and two of these, in particular, can provide the general moral principle that we are seeking because they are implicit within our European cultural heritage and are formulations that we would all recognise. These are as follows:

1. TREAT PEOPLE AS ENDS, NEVER AS MEANS.
2. ACT SO THAT THE MAXIM OF YOUR ACTION CAN BE A UNIVERSAL LAW.

These need a little explanation. 'Treat people as ends, never as means', claims that people are important — one should *never* 'use' people as a means to some other end. Each person is of great value, he or she is 'an end' in his or herself. In religious terms, this might be expressed by saying that each person is 'holy' — although there is no need to be religious in order to recognise this principle.

As soon as a person uses people, he or she debases their value as human beings, they are no longer treating them as human persons but as objects which can be manipulated for their own ends. Each of us is entitled to consideration and respect. Our interests must be considered and we must never be used as tools for someone else's personal interest. This applies whether or not we are famous, wealthy and influential or poor and apparently of little account.

Machiavelli, of course, would not accept this. To him, individuals did not matter — the end was political power and once this was achieved the mass of people had to be kept happy in order that the rulers could hold onto power. Considering other people was unnecessary except in so far as it helped to keep power. Individuals were of no importance in their own right.

The Utilitarians, also, would not accept this. They aimed for the greatest happiness for the greatest number and if the interests of a small minority had to be sacrificed so that the majority could enjoy more pleasure, then so be it. The moral rule 'treat people as ends, never as means' rejects this. It holds that it is *never* permissible to use some group of people — or even one person — as a means for securing the happiness of a wider group.

Real equality, on this view, lies in respecting people — in respecting individuals. Each person, no matter how intelligent or unintelligent, no matter what her colour or creed, no matter how hard working or lazy, no matter how affluent or poor deserves to be treated as a person and should not be 'used'. To be sure, they may have to be restrained, they may have to be put in prison if their activities are sufficiently anti-social — but they must not be used.

The second formulation of the Categorical imperative listed above is 'Act so that the maxim of your action can be a universal law'. This demands that, in any situation, we should act in such a way that we can will (or wish) that the general rule according to which we act should apply to everyone else faced by the same circumstances.

Let us take an example. Imagine that you are faced with a particular moral problem — for instance, should you lie to your customer about what the product you are selling can do. The Categorical imperative asks whether you can sincerely wish that *everyone*, if faced by the same situation, should act in the same way that you are proposing to act. Can you, in other words, wish that all suppliers should lie to their customers if they can get away with it? The obvious answer is that you cannot will this. If you did, you would be willing that *your* suppliers should lie to you about their products when it suited them. If business worked on this basis, trade would come to a halt. No-one could ever trust anyone and commercial relations would break down.

Kant's view of the irreducible importance of individuals, his emphasis on the importance of each human being and the denial that people should ever 'use' others for their own ends provides a possible way forward for business morality. There are few real weaknesses. One may be that the Categorical imperative does not provide specific guidelines for action. Reason and morality are directly linked, but it may not be clear what course of action reason may require in any circumstances. Opinions may, indeed, differ. This, however, need not be seen as a problem. In the real world in which businessmen and women live, simple solutions are often suspect. In a changing world a more dynamic view of morality is required — and this Kant provides. Where issues are ambiguous, further thought and reflection is required. This, surely, is as it should be.

Effectively, Kant's view can be summed up by saying:

PEOPLE MATTER, THEY ARE IMPORTANT. TREAT OTHERS AS YOU EXPECT TO BE TREATED.

This should be the fundamental ground rule for any morality of business. Like most moral judgements, it cannot be proved to be true. However its truth rests on our common cultural heritage. If someone seriously says:

Why should I respect others? Why should I not tread on them and use them as I wish if this will help me to make more money or to build up my company?

Then I want to maintain that everyone would recognise this as an unacceptable position. It is on a par with the other moral positions which, again, we cannot prove but which our common heritage assures us are right (such as not molesting children or not attacking old women).

Anyone who refuses to accept this, we reject without further debate.

In the film *Wall Street*, the arbitrageur, Ghecco, was uninterested in people — they did not matter to him in the slightest. All that mattered was making money for himself and increasing his own power and influence — others were to be considered only in so far as they contributed to that end. He was, although he probably did not know it, in the same philosophic camp as Machiavelli and he deserved to be rejected on similar grounds. He manipulated and 'used' everyone — even those who were closely associated with him. Finally he was brought down by people who turned on him, who recognised him for what he was and who refused to be manipulated.

It is interesting that this general rule has much in common with New Testament morality. Christian morality resists an undue emphasis on rules, although churches have continually tried to make rules the basis for their religion. Instead Jesus summed up the approach to morality taken in the New Testament by saying 'LOVE YOUR NEIGHBOUR AS YOURSELF'. In other words, he called his followers to treat others in the same way that they would like to be treated. 'Treat others as you expect to be treated' is directly in line with this approach, yet it is an approach with which atheist, agnostic, Jew, Hindu, Sikh or Muslim could equally identify.

Although Kant talked in terms of duties, his formulation can also be regarded as enshrining basic human rights. If we have duties to treat others in a certain way, it follows that we have a right to expect to be similarly treated. Each individual, as a human being and irrespective of colour, sex, creed or nationality, has certain inalienable rights. Many of these rights are set out in the 1948 United Nations Declaration of Human Rights and in the earlier American and French Declarations. The rights to life, liberty and the pursuit of happiness as well as the so-called 'economic rights' are part of what it is to be a human being. Any individual must be free to claim these rights for him or herself and anyone in business must never act in such a way as to infringe these rights — whether in dealings with employees, customers, suppliers, shareholders or others.

So far, therefore, we have established a general principle of morality which everyone can accept even though different individuals may think this principle is justified or validated in different ways. We must now turn to see how it can be applied in practice.

Summary

The Machiavellian principle that any means are justified in order to obtain the end one seeks (for instance profit or success) is not an acceptable basis for business morality. The search for happiness, put forward by the Utilitarians, is also illusory and personal intuition is an unreliable guide. Our common European cultural heritage provides a general principle which can ground morality because we can all accept it, even if there is no way of proving it to be true. This principle is: 'People matter, they are important. Treat others as you expect to be treated.'

This has much in common with Christian injunction to 'love your neighbour' although is not dependent on it. It enshrine basic rights of all human beings as well as our duties to others. No businessman or woman should act so as to infringe these rights.

Chapter Five

A QUESTION OF PRIORITIES

In the previous chapter, we saw that our common European cultural heritage has provided at least one general principle that everyone should, if they share our common view of morality and are not amoral, be able to share. The question we now need to ask is whether this general principle is going to be any use at all in resolving moral tensions that occur within a business.

Any businessman or woman knows that there are many forces operating within his or her company or group and these forces can sometimes conflict. Many moral issues within the business world are not straightforwardly 'right' or 'wrong', but rest on a balancing of different priorities in which the interests of one group may affect the competing interests of another. It is rarely possible for everyone to have what they want.

In the US and Europe, there is an increasing tendency for large corporations to adopt lofty 'aims statements' which are intended to set out, in succinct form, the aspirations of the corporations. These aims statements might include paragraphs on the following lines.

1. The directors have an obligation to maximise their company's profitability. This means that the company should seek to obtain business from others in order to increase market share, as well as to maximise margins and reduce costs. The directors have a responsibility to increase the value of the company's shares and to ensure a steadily rising income stream by way of dividends to shareholders.

The company is owned by the shareholders and directors must not forget this.

2. The manager has a responsibility to keep costs as low as possible. This means buying at the lowest possible price consistent with acceptable quality and ready availability; keeping labour costs competitive and making use of the latest hardwear to increase efficiency; eliminating unprofitable lines and utilising property assets to best effect.

3. Employees have a responsibility to carry out the tasks for which they are employed honestly, effectively and well. They have a responsibility to represent their company to the best of their abilities and to carry out their company's policies.

4. The company has a duty to employees, to treat them fairly and to remunerate them properly for the work they do.

5. The company has a duty to its customers — to provide goods and services of known quality and to rectify faults if they occur.

6. The company has a responsibility to suppliers — to deal with them fairly and honestly.

7. The company has a responsibility to the community in which it lives and of which it forms an important part. It has a duty not to pollute the environment to the detriment of others and it has a wider civic duty to be interested in and care for the community in which it operates.

These vague, worthy paragraphs are, to a superficial extent, inspiring. Unfortunately they are not a great deal of use as they are so non-specific.

The various aims set out above can also conflict. Perhaps putting in tight controls against pollution may cost a great deal of money. There may be a choice to be made between polluting a river and decreasing, or even eliminating, profits. Perhaps tighter pollution controls can only be achieved by installing automatic machinery which may mean a reduction in jobs; perhaps the directors' responsibility to maximise the value of the company's shares may lead them to close a factory in an area of high unemployment throwing many people out of work; perhaps an employee's duty of loyalty to the company may conflict with his or her own feelings of moral responsibility — yet the individual may know that to speak out invites dismissal or, at the least, that promotion will be withheld.

In the case of moral tensions between, say, environmental protection and profits, the force of the former can be expected to be less than if legal sanctions were involved. It is not surprising, then, that the moral obligation not to pollute the environment is often not taken seriously and legal sanctions are necessary — resulting, yet again, in the moral imperative being replaced by legal rules.

Nowhere is this balance of forces clearer than in the board room. Here the company's overall policy is, or should be, established. Here the tensions between different priorities should be discussed. Too often, however, the different priorities that a company should have are not even considered — instead there is one god, and that is profit: one arbiter of success, and that is the share price.

To an extent, the culture in which we operate today encourages this position. Most larger groups of companies are quoted on one or more of the world's stock exchanges. The directors know that they control their groups only so long as they perform well. If an outsider believes that the company's assets can be used to better effect, there will be a takeover.

We are increasingly living in a single financial world. The major international financial centres are spaced round the globe so that, at any time, at least one and normally two of these centres are operating. Prices in the different centres are flashed round the world immediately they alter. An entrepreneur in Sydney or Taipei may be looking out for investment opportunities in any part of the world. He can buy or sell companies without leaving his office. He will have analysts constantly researching the share structure of major corporations, looking for a block of shares that may put him in a strong position to act as an 'arbitrageur' — this term merits explanation.

A company may have different classes of voting shares (only the voting shares carry rights to control the destiny of the company — the votes give the power to alter the board and to effect other changes). Once one company controls 50.01 per cent of the votes of another, the second company has been taken over and must follow the directions of the first. It becomes a subsidiary.

In practice, however, because many small shareholders do not vote, a smaller stake is all that is required in order to ensure effective control. It is for this reason that Stock Exchange rules prohibit more than 29.99 per cent of the voting shares of one company being bought by another without the launch of a full takeover bid (this is to prevent Company A buying 35 per cent of Company B, exercising effective control through this stake, and leaving the remaining shareholders to their fate.) Once the magic 30 per cent figure is passed, the Stock Exchange rules require that a full bid must be launched by Company A at the price paid for the most recent purchase of shares — thus giving *all* shareholders the opportunity to share in the benefits of a takeover.

An arbitrageur is an individual or company which seeks to take a strategic stake in another company with a view to selling this stake on to some other organisation which will use it as a spring-board for a full bid. The arbitrageur will seek as large a stake as possible compatible with not pushing up the share price too much. A stake of anything between 5 per cent and 29.9 per cent might be suitable, although most arbitrageur's operate with 10 to 20 per cent stakes. Such a stake would be a crucial first step for anyone contemplating a bid.

The international arbitrageur, therefore, sits in his office and analyses groups of companies round the world — looking for under-utilised assets or, perhaps, for a large company that could be 'broken up' into smaller sections and where the sum of the value of the smaller sections would be larger than the value placed on the conglomerate (a conglomerate is a large group with interests in many different fields).

It is not surprising, therefore, that directors have, as a major preoccupation, their companies' share price and whether they are vulnerable to a takeover bid. No company is so large that it may not be vulnerable. The Kuwait Investment Office built up a 22 per cent stake in British Petroleum — one of the world's largest oil companies — and was forced, by British government action, to disinvest (i.e. to reduce its holding) down to below the 10 per cent level. If BP can be vulnerable, there is no company in the world that can regard itself as immune. Even ICI, Britain's largest company with profits of over £1 100 000 000 a year might, analysts maintain, be worth more if it was broken up into a series of smaller companies. The consequences of such takeovers are dealt with in more detail in Chapter 11.

Given this preoccupation, directors often forget that there are other factors at issue. They instead concentrate on remaining in control and they often do this by devoting all their energies to short-term profitability.

Richard Branson, the entrepreneurial head of the Virgin group, floated his highly successful records to condoms to airline group in 1987. The initial enthusiasm for the issue did not, however, survive the 'great stockmarket crash' of October 1987 and in 1988 Branson decided to buy back the shares issued at the issue price, which was well above the then prevailing market price. He had come to the conclusion that the pressures that went with being a public company were simply not worth the disadvantages. For most large groups, of course, this is not possible.

When considering, therefore, the different priorities that a business has to face, the first step is to recognise that there *are* different forces at work — and that moral responsibilities form a crucial part of these forces.

In some cases, of course, a company's interest in making

profits and its moral obligations may coincide. Levi-Strauss is an example of a company that claims a strong moral basis for its operations. The Hans family took over Levi-Strauss and converted it into a private company. In 1988, it sacked a top manager whose division had achieved outstanding productivity and profit gains. He was fired because he had created a sweatshop atmosphere which was considered to be immoral. The company decided that its employees' welfare came before the drive for ever higher profits. This is, of course, an excellent situation — and Levi-Strauss is a company which has found that having a high moral tone pays dividends. If this is, indeed, the result then there is no conflict between commercial and moral pressures. The real problems arise when these do conflict.

Business ethics is a sea of conflicting pressures. The individual and company is at the centre of a net of forces — many legal and some moral — and deciding between them is rarely easy. Tensions are present all the time, not just between different obligations but between personal promotion, advancement and reward on the one hand and moral duty on the other. The person who succeeds in business, who gets promoted and does well is generally the person who produces results, who increases sales and maximises profits — not the person with the most sensitive moral conscience. The Levi-Strauss manager is an example who is newsworthy because he is an exception to this general rule.

If any worthwhile basis for business morality is to be developed, it must be able to take these tensions into account and to show how they may be resolved. In the absence of this, academics and others who talk about business morality are largely indulging in rhetoric which will be of little relevance in the market place. When I talk to theologians and philosophers who write in this field, it sometimes saddens me that so few have any experience of the world of business. It is not easy running a small or large company, and the academic making profound noises from the sidelines can easily be dismissed by the team on the field who may come to the conclusion that he does not understand what it is like in the pack!

In our general principle ('People matter, they are important. Treat others as you expect to be treated'), both parts of the statement need to be taken together. It is easy to imagine someone taking the second part only and saying, in a moment of frankness to a close friend after a few drinks:

> I expect other people to tread on me if they get half a chance so see my task as being to tread on them first. No-one has ever done me a favour in business and I don't see why I should do anyone else a favour. I'm out for me and, after that, my company — by helping my company to succeed, I will prosper my own interests as well. Sometimes it may help profits or good employee relations (and that, also, helps profits) if I appear to be concerned about moral principles, and then you will find me at the forefront of concern for any popular issues that attract publicity. My basic motto, however, can be summed up by saying 'TO HELL WITH THE LOT OF THEM!'*

If people do, indeed, matter; if they are important, then it cannot be legitimate to derive the motto 'To hell with the

---

* The motto 'To hell with the lot of them' is not my invention. It was the expression my father used after a hard day dealing with trying people at the office. He was, in fact, a gentle and unselfish man, and did not tread on others, but he recognised that he was in a jungle and survival was paramount. Being considerate to others is not easy if one is to succeed in business. He was a director and chairman of various companies within the Unilever and Beecham groups of companies and he had no real friends in either group. Certainly there were plenty of acquaintances, plenty of dinner parties when 'friends' arrived for the evening and professed to have enjoyed themselves, but no 'real' friends. His only real friends were amongst those with whom he swam early every morning in the Serpentine in Hyde Park and who came from very different walks of life. Most of the 'friends' entertained to dinner were confined to the business arena only and the friendship depended on my father being useful. (The relationship between acquaintances in business and real friends is explored in my book *and if it's true?* (Marshall Pickering 1988.)

lot of them' from the last part of our general principle: '. . . treat others as you expect to be treated'. The principle must be looked at as a whole. If the first part is taken into account then we must be considerate about other people, we must not simply tread on them when convenient — even if the cost of such an attitude is high.

It follows from this that, in the nexus of forces which the businessman or woman has to balance, profit or personal or corporate self-interest cannot be the single, over-riding goal. Many companies believe that their sole duty is to make profits and everything else takes second place. Professor Milton Friedman summed this view up when he said:

> The one and only social responsibility of business is to increase its profits.

Others disagree with this, however. Dayton Hudson, the US dry goods chain, has tripled its sales and nearly tripled its profits in the last eight years, but it takes a very different view to that put forward by Milton Friedman. The constitution of the company includes the following:

> The business of business is serving society, not just making money.

Control Data, Johnson & Johnson, NCR, Deere and Company, Motorola and MacDonalds are amongst those which have identified with this view. They all start from the premise that no distinction must be made between the morality of the company and individual morality. This certainly does not mean that they are indifferent to profit, but they are not ready to put profit alone into the driving seat. Dayton Hudson's constitution continues by expressing the position as follows:

> Profit is our reward for serving society well. Indeed profit is the means and the measure of our service — but not an end in itself.

The importance of these final words 'Profit is not an end in itself' cannot be over-emphasised. Once profit becomes the end, then Machiavelli's principle is put in control — everything is acceptable provided it is a means to this end. The difference in approach between the two methods can be illustrated by an example quoted in *The Economist* on 2nd July, 1988.

Cummins Engine, a maker of heavy diesel engines in Columbus, Indiana, has long been famous for its high moral sense. It was one of the first companies to have black senior managers and it allocates 5 per cent of its post-tax profits to charity. A customer of the company, knowing how sensitive it was to moral issues, said to the company that he assumed that Cummins' engines caused less pollution than those of its competitors. Cummins had to confess that their engines were 'not a whit' less dirty. The company's engineers had told the Board that cleaner engines would burn more fuel, be less reliable and cost more. However Cummins did not leave the matter there.

The directors decided that they had a social responsibility to produce engines that gave out less pollution. The company surprised congressmen in Washington by lobbying for stricter anti-pollution standards so that Cummins could produce a cleaner engine without putting itself at a competitive disadvantage. This tactic would protect the interests of shareholders (as Cummins' cleaner engines would be no less efficient than other, environmentally acceptable engines). Cummins also has the benefit of securing valuable publicity at little cost.

If, therefore, profit and morality are not in tension, the company may be able to have the best possible situation. The real difficulties arise where there is a tension between the different forces operating on a company, its directors and employees and where these are not simply resolvable.

Profit is, without doubt, vital — in the absence of profit a company will fail, there will be no funds for research and development, no growth, no further investment, no expansion and no hope for the future. Profit cannot be a dirty word — there is nothing about which to be ashamed in making profits. However the profit motive, by itself, cannot resolve business problems. We cannot, like Machiavelli, be willing to sacrifice all moral principles on the altar of the results we seek. A balance is required. Profit is an important ingredient but so are people and both must be taken into account.

Even if our general principle is read as a whole, however, how is it to be applied? How is the businessman or woman to react when tensions arise between the interests of some individuals or groups of people and the profitability of the company? A choice must often be made — sometimes it is just not possible to get the best of both worlds. This issue is at the heart of most discussions of business morality and will be examined in the succeeding chapters from varying perspectives.

Summary
The businessman or woman faces a variety of different pressures and demands. Any individual in business cannot allow his own or the company's actions to be dominated solely by personal or corporate self-interest or by profits alone. If the principle 'People matter, they are important, treat others as you expect to be treated' is taken seriously, then the last part cannot be isolated from the first. The rights of individuals must be included in the forces that the businessman or woman has to take into account. The tricky problem comes in balancing the different demands.

Chapter Six

THE COMPANY AND
THE EMPLOYEE

A new Rolls-Royce Silver Spur, finished in pale green with matching Connelly leather interior, eases out of the dealers' workshop. It is the afternoon of July 31st, and the car is due for delivery to Simon Jackson, a senior barrister, the following morning with its new licence plate. Payment of the £94 680 (including road fund licence and a full tank of petrol) will be made by banker's draft. The car has been on order for six months and the garage has already registered it from the following morning.

The garage has been through difficult times recently. Profits per unit on Rolls-Royce cars are high and the servicing side of the business is very profitable, but the number of cars sold is small. The garage premises are spacious and are set in the most expensive part of the city. Overheads are substantial. The bank has expressed concern and the directors are worried — although they think they can keep their heads above water.

The mechanic carefully washes the car and then polishes it, ready for delivery the next morning. He gets into the driving seat, first positioning paper covers to protect the leather and the fine Wilton carpet, and reverses towards the garage. However, the entrance is tight, his attention wanders for a moment as a pretty girl passes the showroom and he dents and badly scrapes the driver's side door on a small post which he did not see. He gets out, appalled, to inspect the damage.

The managing director is called and realises the consequences. Mr Jackson is a hard man, he will not accept a damaged car nor will he tolerate a repaired new car. He will simply refuse delivery. The car is now registered and cannot, therefore, be sold as new to someone else. If it is sold second-hand, a loss of up to £20 000 could occur — this, taken with the general problems the company has been having, could prejudice the garage's survival.

There is only one course open. The mechanics will have to work all night. They will fill the dent that has been made and respray the door. When Mr Jackson collects the car it will appear perfect and he will take delivery. However, the managing director knows that, about a week later, signs of the repair will show through. It simply is not possible to fill and respray a dent satisfactorily within 18 hours. Time is required. Once Mr Jackson has taken delivery, the car will be his — there will be no going back. The managing director will tell service reception to express surprise and horror when, as is inevitable, Mr Jackson brings the car in. The garage will, of course, offer to carry out the repair properly at no cost to the owner. All will be well — in particular, Mr Jackson, having taken delivery, will have paid in full and will not be able to reject the car.

* * *

Company directors and managers will sometimes describe their employees' position in terms of these employees working for the company in return for a wage packet or salary cheque. The conditions of this employment, it may be held, are laid down when employees join the company. The level of pay can be altered as the company deems appropriate each year or at regular intervals. The employee has a duty to serve the company to the best of his or her ability and if he or she does not like the conditions, there is nothing to prevent resignation.

This is, however, far too simplistic an account and it does not recognise the complexities of an employee's position. Theoretically it may be true that an employee joins a company knowing what is expected and what the rewards will be, but in practice this is seldom the case. Most new employees have only a rough idea of the job they will be asked to do and they learn 'on the job'. Also company policies and management change over the years; one company may take over another; circumstances in the market place may alter and any employee will constantly find him or herself being faced with new situations.

In many companies, there may be one or more unions that represent workers. If this is the case, workers will often find it easier to take a moral stand as, if the stand is reasonable, there is far less chance of them being singled out and victimised. This will only tend to apply in the larger companies.

The majority of people are employed by small companies where there is no union representation and where commercial pressures are greater — both on the company and on the employee. Also, by and large, unions do not see their role as being moral guardians of the companies with which they are involved. Their task is to improve the lot of their members — to increase wages, better working conditions and improve fringe benefits. Unions can hardly be regarded as the conscience of companies. Indeed with their block votes, less than democratic procedures (at least in many unions) and clear political affiliations — which do not always accord with the views of many of their members — there are moral questions that unions themselves need to consider.

Employees have rights as well as duties, and one of these rights is that they should not be victimised for standing up against immoral or illegal practices.

1. Obedience to law versus obedience to management

Clearly a company cannot expect employees to owe it a sole and over-riding duty of loyal obedience. At the very lowest level, the employee cannot be expected to break the law at the behest of company management. If a tension arises between an obligation to the company and breach of the law, the employee will have the right to insist on not breaking the law. In practice, however, there may be cases when the employee does not choose to exercise this right.

Imagine you are a lorry driver and you live in an area of high unemployment. A vacancy is advertised for a driver and you are taken on. The firm you are working for is small and it has a struggle to survive against the major carriers. You may be asked to drive a lorry that is loaded beyond its safety limit. The lorry may be rated, say, at 38 tons, and on a particular day you may know that the weight is over 40 tons. Straightforwardly, you have the right and the duty not to break the law — you can refuse to drive the lorry until the weight is brought within the legal limits. This is even more clearly the case as, if you are stopped and checked, it is your licence that may be at risk. However if you take this stance, you are quite likely to lose your job — tender consciences are all very well for successful and profitable firms, but for small and struggling concerns in an intensely competitive industry it is not so easy.

Here there are two obligations that are in tension — the one a call to obey the law and the other to comply with the requirements of the company. The decision will rest with each individual and the position will not be clear cut. There are various factors that may have to be taken into account and these may include:

(i) Will the over-loading of the lorry make it potentially dangerous? Clearly if the over-loaded lorry is likely to be unsafe, then the lives of innocent road users are put at risk and this cannot be acceptable. An old, poorly maintained 38-ton lorry loaded to 40 tons might well be unsafe, whereas a new vehicle might have no difficulties at all coping with the excess weight. The driver would have to decide for himself. Naturally he would have to be very cautious before agreeing to drive a vehicle ladened over the limit and he would have to take into account the potential risks he runs in terms of loss of licence. However to say that he should *never* do so may be too simplistic.

(ii) What will happen if the driver refuses to drive the vehicle? If the driver will merely lose some earnings as a result, then this is clearly an unacceptable reason for breaking the law. If, however, his job is put at risk if he refuses to drive then the position becomes at least debatable.

If the driver is a family man and if he is working in an area where there are no other jobs, then the dilemma becomes much more real and he will have to give great thought to his decision. Fortunately in a country like Britain (less clearly so in the US) this is not likely to happen as legislation is in force to protect against improper dismissal — however even in Britain this has been a fairly recent innovation and there may still be cases when an employee may feel vulnerable.

Generally, breach of the law should always be resisted by the employee and should never be morally acceptable. However it is particularly necessary to recognise that where the safety or best interests of others are not placed at risk and the consequences of breaking the law would be extreme (for example, where an employee's job is in an area of high unemployment and when he has a dependent family) personal reflection may be required.

2. Obedience to conscience versus obedience to management

The conflict between the law and an obligation to a company is, however, an extreme case which is rarely going to arise in practice. Much more common will be the cases where the company asks the employee to behave in ways that he or she may consider questionable or unacceptable, although they are perfectly legal. Take the following examples (all of which are based on practical situations experienced by friends of mine):

(i) A carpenter works on a building site. He has been trained to work to a high standard but his employer insists that he uses the cheapest materials and finishes the work in a shoddy way (as this is quicker). The result will be covered by a coat of paint and so the buyer will not know for several years. In another job, he is working to renovate a house and finds dry rot in one of the walls. He knows this will spread quickly and be very serious. However he is told to paper over the problem and disguise the situation with a coat of paint so that the developer can sell on the property and make a quick profit.

(ii) A car mechanic is told to 'patch up' a car ready for resale through the auctions. He knows there is a major engine fault, but there are procedures that he can follow which will hide this for a short period.

(iii) A farm worker is told to spray his employer's fields with heavy concentrations of fertiliser. The levels being sprayed are within the legal limits, but he knows that the nearby river is being heavily polluted by an accumulation of fertilisers and he recognises that he is contributing to this by the spraying operation.

(iv) An office worker is told to delay payment for goods supplied until the last possible moment to improve the company's cash flow. He is told to make excuses if creditors telephone such as saying that the cheque signatories are on holiday or that the cheque has been lost in the post, even though he knows that these statements are not true.

(v) An insurance salesman is told to approach customers and to sell them a restricted range of life insurance policies. As an example, two friends of mine — a clergyman and his wife — were befriended over the years by an insurance salesman who sold them various policies. They eventually inherited £30000 and decided to use it to buy a retirement house for £35000. They would have to borrow £5000 but they were prepared to do this. The insurance salesman advised them that they should take out a mortgage of £25000 and invest £20000 in a special 'deposit bond' with his company. The interest from this would pay the mortgage interest. Only later did they discover that the insurance salesman made £1000 of commission by this transaction and that it was very poor investment advice.

In all these cases the employee is being asked to behave immorally. The situation described in (v) is different from the remainder as the insurance salesman did not have to give this specific advice and he is getting a major personal financial benefit from acting in this way. Such action is wrong and to be deplored. He is putting personal profit before any moral sense and is going directly against the general moral principle outlined in the previous chapter.

In the first four scenarios the employee receives no direct benefit himself, yet he is being asked to work in ways that are contrary to what he considers to be right. However the proposed actions are not illegal. He cannot claim the protection of the law and, if he fails to carry out the work, others will soon be found to do it. This last is not an excuse for immoral behaviour. Guards at Aushwitz and Treblinka might have used the same defence — many Nazis were convicted at the Nuremburg war crimes trials even though they claimed that they were obeying orders.

The above cases are only the tip of the iceberg. Employees are constantly asked by at least some employers to act immorally. Most employees do not even realise that they need to make a decision — they simply do what they are told. Yet this, in itself, is a decision. It may be that the manager or director who has asked the employee to act in this way is not even being immoral — what is and is not immoral is not always clear cut. As we shall see shortly, there may be good reasons for the type of behaviour outlined being necessary.

How can our general principle help in the sorts of situation outlined above? There seem to be no clear cut answers. Certainly it rules out the example of the insurance salesman's action — the salesman could not will that he should be treated in the way that he was treating the clergyman and his wife, nor was he regarding those who looked on him as a friend as being important individuals in their own right. Our general principle merely confirms the instinctive rejection we feel towards the salesman's action.

There is no hard and fast answer in the first four cases — and perhaps this is as it should be. The individual will have to make a personal decision having weighed up the alternatives. When Kant formulated his 'Categorical imperative', he declined to give firm rules for moral action as 'circumstances alter cases'. He denied that there were absolute rules that would apply in every situation. Similarly in the examples we have looked at, the individual employee's reaction to the situation will vary depending on the circumstances, the community in which the individual lives and the position of the company.

Someone may well argue that this approach is unduly pragmatic. Academics, in particular, do not like a pragmatic approach to morality — they prefer moral systems that are clear cut. However real life is seldom like that.

It may be useful to put forward a list of factors that an employee should consider before carrying out instructions that he or she regards as being ethically doubtful. This list cannot be comprehensive as it is impossible to envisage every possible situation, nor will the answers necessarily provide a clear decision. The problem of morality within business is that it *is* a problem — not to be resolved lightly by over-simple rules. Anyone who actually works in business, will know that easy answers are an illusion. The list of factors might be as follows:

(1) Would anyone be likely to be hurt by the proposed action who could not be expected to be aware of the risks and, therefore, who should have made relevant enquiries before entering into the transaction?

(In the case of the purchase of a car by auction, it might reasonably be held that the watchword is *Caveat Emptor* — let the buyer beware. By buying at auction any individual is taking a risk and hoping to pay less for a vehicle than if it was bought through a recognised garage.)

(2) Is the person who is likely to be hurt well able to afford the loss or in a position to foresee the various possibilities?

(The insurance salesman's action in (v) above was to be condemned partly because he was selling to a couple who trusted him and who had no specialised knowledge. If he had been selling to a qualified accountant, the same criteria would not apply.

If any employee is being called on to deceive a customer, then the employee may have a more tender conscience if the deception will result in a loss to someone who cannot afford it, whereas if the person could well afford the loss, then a high moral position may not be so urgent.)

(3) Will refusal to carry out the action result in the loss of the employee's job? If so, are there other jobs available?

(Selfish motives are not, generally, good guides to conduct. However an individual does owe a moral duty to family as well as to company. In areas where unemployment may run as high as 30 per cent and where there are few alternative jobs or where dependent children suffer because social security benefits are too low to allow a reasonable standard of living — then it is not unreasonable that an individual must take moral responsibility to family into account when deciding whether to take the high moral ground and thus lose his or her job.)

(4) Is the type of practice being proposed the norm in the industry concerned?

(In the building industry, it may be accepted — unfortunately — that poor quality workmanship is more common than not. No farm worker can reasonably expect to have a tender conscience about applying heavy doses of fertiliser, since this is a practice that is accepted by a majority of farmers within Europe and America. He or she may not like it, but this practice is a fact of life.

In either case, if an employee feels sufficiently strongly about the position, then resignation may be the best alternative — although it must be recognised by the individual who does this that there are so few jobs in, say, farming that the chances of working for a farmer who does not use fertiliser are not high.)

(5) Will the proposed moral stand make any difference at all? If the stand will result in dismissal and the work will be carried out by someone else, then this must be taken into account in the decision.

(This is a difficult criterion. If everyone accepts that an illegitimate practice is inevitable and co-operates with 'the system', then no changes will ever be made. However this must be balanced against the individual's wider moral responsibilities to family and to community. This will demand an assessment of each individual case.)

If these criteria were applied, then it *may* seem reasonable for the 'immoral' action to be carried out by the employee in all the situations outlined in (i) to (iv) above, if he or she is requested to do this by a manager or director. The final decision only the employee can make.

3. An employee's duty to the company

So far we have considered the situation where the employee is asked, by the company, to do something that he considers to be immoral. Another set of problems arise — although these are easier to resolve — if we consider the employees' duty to the company.

Many employees do things which may well be considered immoral if they are looked at closely. They draw petrol, supposedly for company use, and use it for personal purposes; they photocopy private documents on the company machine; they take stationery — paper, pens, typewriter ribbons — for use at home; they over-change for travel on company business; they charge overtime which has not been worked; they take days off saying they are sick to watch a football match or to take part in their favourite hobby; they short-cut jobs that they are meant to do thoroughly in order to earn a bonus — the list is almost endless and these practices occur in every company in the country. Are these practices morally acceptable?

Again, the position is not necessarily clear cut. Much depends on whether the practice is openly sanctioned or whether it has to be clandestine. A good rule of thumb, following the pragmatic, consequentialist approach to morality on which we have embarked, may be to a see whether the practice in question is known to and sanctioned by the managers to whom the employee is responsible. In the case, say, of falsification of overtime returns or over-charging for business travel, official sanction will almost never be given. It is true that some companies may permit first-class travel to be charged by an employee and may countenance the employee travelling tourist class and, say, taking his wife or her husband on the trip. Such behaviour, if openly approved, is not immoral. However, almost invariably falsification of returns is immoral and is to be rejected because it is not approved.

The situation is less clear with, say, the moderate use of a firm's photocopier or telephone for private purposes. Again much may depend on whether this practice is sanctioned by the manager or not and whether the use is 'moderate'. For an employee to come in during the evening, to avoid being seen, and to copy a huge manuscript for a friend, is another matter entirely.

It may not be sufficient for a manager to know and approve certain practices for them to be regarded as moral. Some managers are weak and acquiesce to dubious procedures, other companies — faced, perhaps, by strong union pressure — are forced to agree to practices which verge on the immoral. Such practices occurred in Fleet Street print rooms before most of the national newspapers broke the stranglehold of the print Chapters. In the 'old' days, some employees would only work for a few hours a night and yet would earn enormous salaries — often far in excess of the journalists'. Jobs on certain newspapers were passed on from father to son and management were almost forbidden to manage. We have here a case of the immoral use of union power — just as in the nineteenth century there were many, many cases of immoral abuse of employer power.

Freedom is a central part of business morality and if management, union or employee freedom is unduly restricted by forces beyond their control, then this may be a less than ideal situation — even though it may be very common.

5. An employer's duty to the employee

At the most basic level, the employer owes a duty of care to the employee. The employee must not be placed in a hazardous position where his or her safety is in danger. This means, for instance, that in a factory industrial safety must be taken seriously. This is particularly the case in industries where injuries are a real problem such as mining or where heavy machinery is being used. Safety standards need to be applied and employees' interests safeguarded. In the case of new products, the materials used must be tested and safety implications evaluated. The new American STEALTH bomber, which is invisible to radar and heat seeking missiles, uses advanced materials and is produced under conditions of great secrecy — but employees are already claiming a high incidence of cancer amongst staff using the new materials.

An example of one less exotic industry where this obligation is not always taken seriously is that of construction. In an eight-week period in 1988, there were eleven deaths in the construction industry in London alone as well as hundreds of injuries. A total of 152 building workers and members of the public died in Britain in the previous year from construction-related accidents and the figure constantly rises. The Construction Safety Campaign considers that the morality of many firms can be summed up in the phrase: 'Your health — Their wealth'. Employees who complain about safety are often sacked whilst management sometimes ensures that as many employees as possible go 'on the lump' — in other words they are treated as self-employed. This means that they can be dismissed easily, costs can be saved and safety considerations ignored. Clearly if profits are put before safety, then this is a morally indefensible position and responsibility for this must be taken by the directors and managers of the companies concerned.

The Health and Safety Executives' five-year report showed that there were more than two deaths every week on construction sites and that 90 per cent of these could have been prevented. In 70 per cent of cases, positive action by management could have saved lives. The three greatest killers were poor maintenance; transport and mobile plant and accidents during demolition and dismantling. The Health and Safety Executive issued more than 1000 prohibition notices, which can only be served when there is a risk of 'serious personal injury', but there were only twenty-five prosecutions. These statistics occurred during a time when the construction industry's profits have been at an all time high and there does seem grounds for the claim that profit is being put before people. This represents a clear moral failure by the employers concerned.

If people do, indeed, matter — as our principle affirms — then a central part of affirming the importance of individual employees is that they should be free and should be encouraged to develop as individuals. We should all be free and should be encouraged to develop as human beings. We should all be free to make decisions about our own lives and we should be able to work in an environment where our talents can be developed. If we take away someone else's freedom merely as a means of profit for our company, then we diminish them as human beings.

A slave is not free, a robot waits to be programmed — a human being, however, cannot and must not be treated in the same way. There are more ways than one, however, of taking away human freedom or diminishing a person's humanity. Giving a person menial, 'soul-destroying' work which requires no thought can be equally de-humanising. Many people are condemned to monotonous, routine work which is boring, repetitive and requires no initiative or thought. More and more companies are, however, recognising that this is unsatisfactory.

In many American and European motor companies in the past, mass production line assembly procedures meant that a person on the line would do the same, routine task day after day. He would have no interest in the finished product and would never see more than a very small part of the assembly line. Volvo, by contrast, pioneered a new procedure whereby each individual worked as part of a small team which was responsible for the production of a complete vehicle. They were responsible for the vehicle they produced and could participate in the whole of the production process. Volvo found that there was a considerable increase in productivity and a far higher quality standard. More and more large US and British companies are now moving towards the same procedure. This not only increases quality and production rates but, more important, it avoids the dehumanisation process that the production line imposes.

The Company and the Employee

Marx rejected capitalism partly because he considered that this system would exploit workers in the interest of profit and this was dehumanising. The capitalist system was claimed to feed off the labour of workers who would always tend to be paid too little and who would not share properly in the results of their efforts. There was, therefore, no alternative but to overthrow the capitalist system and place the means of production in the hands of the workers. The logic of Marx's argument is straightforward — all men are equal, private property is theft and this injustice can only be removed by state ownership.

In practice, of course, in communist countries the state factories are certainly not enlightened and fulfilling places to work — the only attraction they have is that it is very difficult for an employee to get dismissed. However there is little challenge and little chance for self-development. Marx may have been wrong (and certainly the arguments by which he arrived at his conclusions can be challenged philosophically and are based on dubious premises), but many Western companies have seemed determined to prove him right — even if there are now moves to take employees more seriously as human beings.

Edward Deming is not a well known name. He is an American who has worked in Japan since 1950 helping Japanese industry to turn their shoddy, imitative post-war products into some of the highest quality consumer goods in the world. Japan's top industrial award is now called 'The Deming prize' and in 1960 he was awarded one of Japan's highest honours — the first American to receive it. Yet this man is almost unknown in America and Europe. He considers that only 15 per cent of production faults are caused by workers, 85 per cent are due to poor management (his '85–15 rule'). He believes that devotion to quality starts a chain reaction bringing higher productivity, lower costs, more sales, more profits and happier customers and workers — a real virtuous circle. Deming is a blistering critic of Western management styles and believes that a total transformation in attitudes is required to save Western industry from further decline.

Deming has many ardent dislikes including unfriendly takeovers, leveraged buy-outs, pressure for quarterly results, constant performance appraisals and management by objective — all of which have been the most fashionable of management tools in the West in the last fifteen years. His book *Out of the Crisis* published by MIT and Cambridge University Press should be compulsory reading for any businessman who has responsibility for a production unit in Europe or the US. The virtuous circle that he points to is not just a theory, it is something that most Japanese companies have consciously put into practice and it has solid moral benefits in many directions. In many ways it is founded on respect for workers and helping these workers to achieve the best possible results — for themselves as well as for the company of which they come to feel an important and valued part. This is one reason why Deming frowns on hostile takeover bids and constant pressure for short-term performance as opposed to longer-term objectives.

Employees need to be provided with opportunities for self-development by employers providing opportunities to train in new skills, to learn new operating techniques and to be more efficient. Employees need to be valued and treated as an integral part of the company. It is so easy for a company to allow an employee to simply continue in the same way as in the past with no challenge and no possibility of development. If the company's expectations are low, it is not surprising that it will be rewarded by low levels of performance and lack of imagination.

By treating people in this way, companies will normally reap a considerable dividend in terms of greater efficiency and improved quality. On the other hand, the employee reasonably owes a duty of effort and loyalty to the company — it is a reciprocal relationship. The company, however, must see its moral responsibility in active rather than passive terms. Morality is not just about refraining from certain actions, it also demands positive steps to help employees in their development.

Of course, not all employees will respond. Many will not wish to develop or not be capable of taking on more than a certain restricted range of tasks. In the drive for greater efficiency and profitability that the competitive environment demands, the jobs of such employees may be placed at risk.

Mediocrity is not a sin and many companies will be able to find jobs for mediocre individuals which they can perform successfully and well. However, if an individual is unable or unwilling to develop the skills that a company needs and if the company has *genuinely* used its very best endeavours to find suitable employment for the individual at the level at which he or she is capable of working, then if the employee is unable to cope with the task given it must be recognised that employer and employee may have to part company.

Much depends on the genuineness of the efforts made by the company and this is a moral issue. Many employers make little or no effort to develop their employees and, if the employee fails to perform satisfactorily, they will simply seek to dismiss the individual — on whatever legal grounds may be available. There is, therefore, a grey area here. Much will depend on the extent to which the company considers that it really has a moral obligation to each of its employees and is really trying to take the general principle which we have established seriously.

Summary
The ideal employee/company relationship should be one based on freedom and mutual respect, where the rights and opinions of the employee and his or her personal development are seriously taken into account and valued by the employer whilst the employee has a willingly accepted duty and obligation to prosper the interests of the company. The employee is not simply a business tool, used to assist in the

creation of profits. He or she is important in his or her own right and must not be 'used' or treated like an object, as a means to some wider end.

Employees need to be treated as an integral part of the company; their interests and safety need to be safeguarded and they must be helped to participate in the drive for better quality which will help move towards Deming's virtuous circle.

It is a high vision, but any proper appreciation of what it is to respect people, to treat them as human beings who really matter, demands nothing less.

Chapter Seven

THE DIRECTOR
AND THE MANAGER

The 1980s has been the decade of the Yuppies — young city experts who earn enormous salaries. It has not been uncommon for 24 to 30-year-old dealers in City foreign exchange dealing rooms, young merchant bankers and property developers to earn salaries of £30000 to £100000 or more. In the same period, teachers and academics, hospital workers, secretaries and production workers have seen increases in their salaries above the rate of inflation, but still only to levels which rule out the possibility of them being able to buy a house. A recent survey showed that half the young families in the home counties could not afford to buy houses.

Those who owned property at the beginning of the 1980s have seen values treble or more within less than ten years. The 'haves' have gained much more, financially, than they could have dreamed, the 'have-nots' have found themselves slipping further and further away from the good life promised by the 'loads-a-money' society. Many people have held that these inequalities are immoral. In particular, they have criticised the high pay rises given to directors and the poor treatment of lower paid workers.

In order to decide whether the Yuppies and the highly paid directors deserve the money they earn, it is necessary to consider what they do for it and the standards according to which their successes are to be measured.

Managers are the middlemen of business — responsible

to the directors for particular sections of the business operations and, although this is often not recognised, responsible for the employees who are under their control. It is sometimes an unenviable position as there may not be all that much freedom of action and managers are often called on to implement policies or to work towards objectives which they did not establish. Much depends on the tone of the company that is set, ultimately, by the directors.

Managers have to prepare budgets, which are subject to revision by more senior line management or by the directors, and have to comply with these and to try to improve performance — cutting costs and increasing revenues to improve the gross and net margins. The directors normally use financial criteria to monitor the activities and the success or failure of those who work for them. Human criteria are rarely used at all. Not many directors seriously evaluate managers in terms of the way they develop or care for their employees — profit is the sole arbiter of success.

What is success for a company? Almost always this question will be answered in financial terms — in terms of increased profit, better return on investment, improved dividend payments or an increased share price. Rarely will other factors be taken into account, although if the company has an 'aims statement' other factors may be acknowledged. This applies even to those companies where, from the outside, it appears likely that other factors might well be anticipated.

Publishers in the religious field provide a good example. What is the motive that impels these publishers? Certainly they will be concerned with financial success and profit-ability — without profits a company cannot survive and expand. However their aims for their product should, surely, go beyond this.

If religious publishers confine themselves to financial criteria then what they are doing is little different from the manufacturer of sausages or the publisher of tabloid newspapers — their only objective is to produce an attractive sausage or newspaper that will sell and there is no interest in content other than as it affects the sales figures. A religious publisher might be expected, however, to have a wider vision than this and, if there is such a vision, then it needs to be clearly stated to everyone in the company.

In the case of some religious publishers their interest in putting over their 'message' may become so great that it overshadows the need for profits and, in this case, corporate failure is a real possibility. A balance is required but the whole point about a balance is that more than one weight is involved. Finance alone cannot be allowed to be the sole determining factor. A religious publisher who was only interested in the bottom line and who did not treat employees as if they were individuals who mattered in their own right might well be considered to be in a dubious moral position.

One of the crucial tests of a company's moral awareness is whether or not the directors recognise criteria that go beyond the financial in their supervision of managers and employees. These criteria may differ between companies, but many of the most important factors will be the same. The treatment of employees, suppliers, customers, shareholders and the communities in which the company operates are all factors that need to be considered. This book tries to deal with these issues as well as some of the minimum standards that a well managed company that makes any claims to moral integrity should be willing to take seriously. Unlike Machiavelli, such issues cannot be ignored as mere impedimenta on the road to profit. The end cannot justify the means taken to achieve it.

Unfortunately these wider issues are all too rarely taken into account. The sole yardstick for success corporate is often financial, the sole means of measuring performance is the bottom line. Money becomes the new god to whom all managers and employees must make obeisance. It must be the responsibility of directors to woo employees away from this attitude and to show, by example and directive, that whilst profit is vitally important there are other factors that must also be considered. As we shall see later, shareholders also have a responsibility to take wider factors into account. If share holders are only interested in profits and nothing else then it is small wonder that directors feel compelled to ignore wider considerations as well.

Employees within companies which fail to take this wider vision seriously come to realise that their positions are not secure — at any time dismissal is a real possibility. The management's interest in them is restricted to their usefulness in increasing profits. To be sure, this atmosphere of nervousness can in the short term increase productivity and indeed profits, as individuals are driven partly by fear of dismissal. However in the long term it is not a satisfactory recipe either for long term security or, indeed, for financial security and success.

It was a recipe for success common in America in the 1960s and 1970s and is still in widespread use in Europe by managements who are ten years or more out-of-date.Some American companies, by contrast, have now moved to follow Japanese management styles which involve a very much greater commitment to employees. In Japan, employees are traditionally regarded as being in a long-term relationship with the company — the company has a permanent commitment reflected by management's attitudes to its employees. Employees are seldom dismissed, instead they are developed, cared for and fostered with a care and commitment that has been alien to much American and European business.

Some may find the Japanese style restrictive, but the 3000 workers in Nissan's new plant in Sunderland have found it liberating. They are constantly consulted, directors park, eat and go to the toilet in the same place as their employees, the employees are made to feel part of a successful enterprise, all members of which are working on the same side. Salaries are high and there are no time clocks. Such is the dedication of the employees that they all arrive in good time for the beginning of the day, they work as part of small teams and can see the results of their endeavours. Quality standards are exceptionally high and sales of Nissan cars are booming. Production rates are already equal to those in Japan and the Sunderland workers are determined to beat their parent company colleagues — not from any sense of fear but from a sense of pride (Deming's virtuous circle, outlined in the previous chapter, seems to be being achieved).

Japan itself is economically the single most successful country in the world and its people enjoy one of the highest standards of living with the lowest rate of unemployment. This is not a coincidence. The management style and the co-operative nature of Japanese management is distinctive. In Japan, all members of the company are meant to co-operate and pull together — individualism within the company is minimised, but this does not mean that the individual does not matter. Thorough discussion takes place in order to establish a corporate view. Innovation is welcomed as employees know that their jobs are secure — in contrast to Britain and America where innovations and new technology are seen as a threat to jobs. This is because most Western managements have no real commitment to the long-term interests of employees and will be quite ready to make individuals redundant if this is commercially desirable.

Japanese management, by contrast, traditionally felt a moral obligation to employees. Employees knew this and did not, therefore, feel threatened. They knew that the best safeguard for their jobs was the success of their companies — of which they form a vital and valued part. The past tense is used here as there are some indications that the traditional Japanese style is beginning to move more towards the American approach.

Individualism is much more a feature of Western than of the Japanese management approach. There is a sense, in the West, that each person must look out for himself and that one person has little responsibility for another. Partly for this reason, the whole idea of teamwork and pride in the company is foreign to many American and European companies. The sense of corporate belonging that has been such a feature of Japanese companies is alien to Western culture, but this does not mean that Western management cannot learn from the Japanese management style and the importance it attaches to the company's workforce.

These practices are gradually beginning to be taken seriously by European management. More progressive managers are just beginning to see not only the moral worth of treating employees as individuals, but also the bottom line benefits for a company whose directors, managers and employees are working together as a single unit with a co-ordinated objective and with no sense of fear. Ford, General Motors, AT & T and the Campbell Soup Company have all now taken Deming's ideas on board — but the number of such companies is tiny in relation to European and American industry as a whole.

There are, of course, shining examples of British companies that have sought to follow an ethical vision which did not put profit into first place. Cadburys and Rowntrees are good examples — they were founded by Quakers and had the highest standards of care for their employees, although in recent years the aggressive marketing policies of both companies, working as they do in an intensely competitive environment, has led to a falling away from the original vision and an increased emphasis on performance at a cost, sometimes, paid by employees.

Cadbury's Bournville factory was a 'green fields' site where the company developed housing for their employees of a standard unmatched at the time. Their products were of the highest quality and the employees' working environment was excellent. For many generations, the respective families developed their companies with great success and their brand names became familiar around the world. Here, indeed, virtue seemed to be rewarded for many years. However, Rowntrees had to pay the price imposed by financial realities. The family had given up personal control as more financial resources were needed than the family shareholders could provide. This led to the famous takeover battle between Nestlé and Suchard in 1988 which was ultimately won by Nestlé (although with Suchard making a very large profit on its stake in Rowntree). Nestlé was simply willing to pay a higher price than Rowntree's management could justify. The market share of Rowntrees put together with its new parent gave the combined group an international strength that justified an exceptional price tag.

Directors are responsible for establishing the overall direction, purpose and tone of the company. They do not, sadly, always take this seriously. Individually directors may feel vulnerable — all directors are not equal, some are more equal than others. Often a Board is dominated by one or two individuals and any dissent will be suppressed. Some chairmen are careful to ensure that the Board is controlled by individuals who will side with them and they adopt a policy of 'divide and rule'. One of the signs of management weakness making companies vulnerable to corporate failure is where a company has the role of managing director and chairman combined in one person. So much concentrated power means that there are no checks and balances to guard against mistakes or foolish policies.

In theory, the directors are responsible to shareholders, but this is closer to theory than to practice. Shareholders do not generally know much about the company's activities and, provided the performance looks reasonable, will almost never be in a position to question or challenge the way that a company is managed.

It is for this reason that many investors and bankers are

keen to see independent non-executive directors (these are directors, ideally well qualified, experienced and with outside interests, who do not take part in the day-to-day running of the company and who can, therefore, 'stand back' from the situation and be independent) on the boards of companies — so that they can stand up to the chairman and the directors he 'controls' and can consider wider interests than those of the chairman. It is not always easy to find directors of the right calibre and there are relatively few cases of non-executive directors who are willing to take a stand against their colleagues. The Bank of England maintains an unofficial register of suitable members of the 'great and the good' who can act as non-executive directors of larger companies if they are required. Sometimes former senior politicians can fill this role — although whether politicians are the right people to safeguard a company's moral conscience may, perhaps, be a matter for debate!

In the United States, executive directors are responsible to a Board composed largely of non-executives. The executives are not, therefore, entirely their own masters and sometimes the non-executives can take a broader view.

Although it is an ideal, often not met in practice, the directors should establish the direction in which the company is going and lay down the aims and objectives for its operations. They face a heavy responsibility and, more than any other group, have to take into account conflicting pressures. How, then is our general principle ('People matter, they are important. Treat others as you would wish to be treated') to be applied in practice by the manager or director?

There are, of course, two stages involved. The general principle, as the first premise in the argument, may be rejected (although the reasons in favour of it have already been given) but, even if this principle is accepted, the conclusions that are developed from it may be held to be false. Care is needed, therefore, in formulating the conclusions.

The directors have numerous responsibilities:

  (i) to shareholders,
 (ii) to the wider community,
(iii) to suppliers and customers,
(iv) to employees and
 (v) to managers,

as well, of course, to themselves and their families. As with employees, tensions often arise between the director's conscience and his or her other responsibilities. The responsibilities to shareholders, to the wider community and to suppliers and customers will be dealt with in succeeding chapters when the relationship between a company and these groups are discussed. The company's policy is set by the directors so their responsibilities and the company's are considered at the same time.

It is important to consider the directors' relationship with managers and employees. A pre-condition of caring for employees and treating them as human beings is that the company should be healthy and successful. It must be able to sell its goods or services profitably in an increasingly competitive marketplace. Nothing happens unless something is sold — this is too easily forgotten. A company must be able to sell its goods at an adequate net margin — otherwise it will fail. This is likely to involve constant change and development as new competitive pressures are dealt with. The company that does not change and adapt will soon die. The history of commerce is littered with dinosaurs who thought they could rest on their reputation and were overtaken by lean, hungry predators. Indeed, the larger a company grows the more vulnerable it may become to the 'dinosaur mentality'. It may become fat and lazy, full of overheads and unresponsive to changes in the market place. Such companies are doomed unless they can change their ways. It must be one of the paramount duties of directors and senior managers to preserve the 'lean and hungry' approach to business.

Directors, as a matter of good business practice, have to

formulate a plan as to where the company is going and what its objectives are. They will also have to consider how these objectives are to be implemented. We have already seen earlier in this chapter that a well-managed company should have broader objectives than financial success. These objectives should be clear to managers and employees — the company should have a sense of purpose, of moving in a planned direction. If a company has established objectives, the managers should be involved in regular consultations as to whether these are being achieved. Too often, the only consideration given by directors is to their managers' budgets — implying that only financial criteria matter.

A good test to determine whether a company has a clear plan and whether it has been communicated successfully is to ask middle managers of the company whether they have any clear idea of the company's medium-term objectives. Sadly, they will often say that they have no idea at all. Either the directors have failed to formulate a plan or, if they have, it is kept confidential and not communicated to those who will be expected to implement it.

An increasing number, albeit still a small minority, of progressive companies are introducing an annual review policy for employees. Under this arrangement, each manager discusses with the employees who are responsible to him or her their objectives for the following year, how these are to be achieved and the training that will be given to help develop the employees. These are recorded in writing together with the ways that these objectives are to be measured. ('Management by objectives' has made clear to most managers that it is essential to establish measurable criteria for employee performance — although this may not be the ideal model for individual appraisal, as Deming's analysis shows.) Setting objectives should not be seen as a way of providing a stick for managers to use against their employees — this is a wholly negative approach. To be successful, the emphasis must be put on the positive side by trying to help the employee to see how he or she can develop necessary skills and so progress as an individual as well, of course, as benefiting the company.

At the end of the year, the manager discusses the previous year with the employee, evaluating performance against the established objectives and going through a written report on the employee's strengths and weaknesses, how he or she has developed as a result of the challenges of the year, any reports that may have been received from participation in training programmes and other relevant comments. Salary is discussed, rather than any increase just being notified by letter, and the level of increase may be openly related to performance. Everything is open and above board and the employee can comment on the report. The report is included in the employee's personal file and is seen by the manager's boss. If the employee disagrees with anything included in the report, he or she has the right to object in writing and this will be recorded in the file.

This procedure has great advantages from an efficiency point of view and also from an ethical perspective. Each employee is being treated seriously and respected as an individual. He or she knows what is required and has a clear, written report on his or her performance which is discussed and which he or she can object to. Everything is, or should be, out in the open. The employee knows that his or her efforts are appreciated and that training will be given to develop the skills necessary to face new challenges. Above all, the employee feels valued and an important part of the enterprise. Some managers, wrongly, feel embarrassed at discussing performance with employees. However this is to be less than fully open. Again, the responsibility for this lies with the directors who must be prepared to take a decision in favour of 'open management'. Too many companies operate on a 'need to know' basis whereby everything is kept confidential and secret unless details absolutely have to be disclosed. The morally preferable course is a management style that encourages disclosure and discussion unless there are exceptional reasons why this may not be appropriate — for instance, because of an imminent takeover. Managers and employees almost always respond to trust and to openness. If they are not consulted, they are likely to react accordingly.

It is all too easy to build up resentment — sometimes without directors being aware of the position. If the chairman and managing director receive salary increases of 30 per cent and the lower paid workers receive 6 per cent, it is not surprising that a feeling of resentment may begin. These increases, unless clearly explained and justified, appear to say something about the directors' attitude to lower paid staff. Staff are, effectively, being treated as 'cost centres' — they are necessary costs which must be curtailed as far as possible. They are not being looked on as people who are partners in the business in that they provide the labour on which the business depends. Obviously it would be ridiculous for managing director and factory cleaner to receive the same pay — substantial differences are inevitable. It may well be right for the chairman to be paid £100000 and for a cleaner to get £8000. However the directors should be concerned about the cleaners — just as about all other staff — as individuals who matter. They are not just 'cost centres'. They are human beings who must be treated accordingly, who must be paid fairly and on an understandable basis and their efforts rewarded from the success of the business.

Senior business executives are no longer simply paid a large salary — they are now 'compensated'. This can cover a whole variety of additional benefits from perks, bonuses and stock options to, more recently, substantial leaving payments. There has always been a practice of having to 'pay off' the balance of a contract when an unwanted manager or director with a service contract is sacked. However the principle has now been extended. Old directors now get 'compensated' — what for is not always clear. At Kleinwort Benson, a payment of £805000 was shared between two directors who headed off to retirement. The board of tobacco giant, Rothmans, rewarded their 68-year-old chairman a £750000 leaving payment for increasing profits in his three years as chairman — during which the world economy had, in any case, boomed and for which he had been very well paid.

There is nothing wrong with incentives to help all members of a company's staff achieve better results, but the moral justification, in general, for enormous payments to people who are well paid and are going to leave in any case seems obscure — except, possibly, that it establishes a principle from which the directors who approved it can expect to benefit. Directors of really large companies sometimes come to feel that they own the company and that they can do as they wish. Shareholders, if they wished, have the power to show them that the facts are otherwise.

The directors' responsibility *is* heavy and it is right that their success and leadership should be rewarded — but they have a moral responsibility to ensure that the rewards are fair and are not unjustifiably large merely because no-one questions them.

The Yuppie foreign exchange dealer who, at a very early age, is earning an astronomical salary may seem in an odd position to the outsider. However if she is an outstanding FOREX (Foreign Exchange) dealer, she may well earn for her company many times the amount paid to her. The strains of working as a FOREX dealer are considerable and the really good ones are rightly highly paid. To decide whether an 'appropriate' salary should be £30000, £50000 or £100000 is far from straightforward — much will depend on individual judgement and competitive pressures.

If a City bank, operating as it does in a highly competitive environment, wants to recruit the best staff who will generate the highest profit, then it is no good offering lower salaries than the bank next door. The institution that took a moral decision to pay its best staff badly would not remain long in business! The outstanding director or FOREX dealer; the really able property dealer or marketing genius, able to spot and exploit the market opportunity that no-one else sees, brings real benefits to his company from which all employees benefit. The crucial moral question is not how much the managing director is paid but whether the fruits of the company's success (which may have been initiated by the MD but could not have taken place without the rank-and-file workers) have been properly and fairly shared between all the employees of the company.

Multinational companies are sometimes in a strong bargaining position as they can locate new plants and source materials from a variety of different countries. They may have no need, therefore, to pay more than the going rate for labour and, if union pressure in one country tries to secure a larger than acceptable wage rise, production can be switched elsewhere — even though such switches are not straightforward. The moral question that needs to be asked is whether it is right to only pay employees what they 'need' to be paid. To take this view is to treat them as less than fully human, it is to ignore their importance as persons in their own right who have made essential contributions to a company's success and who, therefore, are owed something beyond the minimum necessary.

Too seldom do directors take seriously their duties to and responsibilities for their employees.

When British Leyland was taken over by British Aerospace, thousands of redundancies were announced the day after the deal was concluded, although the chairman and managing director of British Leyland would be on the main board of British Aerospace and could look forward to an exciting future. Some of the workers, interviewed after the redundancies were announced, were bitter that little consideration seemed to be given to them. The redundancies would have been necessary even if the merger had not gone through but their announcement the day after it was concluded did not give this impression to the workforce.

The company with high moral standards will, if it becomes necessary to lay off workers, take their future very seriously. They will consider whether there is any possible way of providing alternative employment, they will consider whether vacancies at other plants might be offered to the redundant employees, they will discuss with government and other organisations the possibility of retraining programmes — in short they will take seriously their moral commitment to their employees. They will specifically *not* be satisfied with 'good severance terms'. Such an attitude treats employees as means to an end — they are not an end in themselves, valued and cared for as individuals even though no longer immediately useful to the company.

There are, rightly, high expectations of the moral leadership that directors and senior managers should provide. One of the key factors that managers and employees expect of their employers is fairness.

When I was chairman of a substantial Mercedes-Benz dealership, the managing director was a tough, wiry individual who had worked his way up from a mechanic. He was not only physically tough — being quite capable of 'facing up' to irate members of the travelling fraternity who were in dispute with a member of staff — but he was tough in other ways as well. He worked hard, getting to the office early and being one of the last to leave. He made considerable demands on employees and was not tolerant of foolishness, laziness or incompetence — but he was respected by employees and also by customers. Above all, he was fair — and known to be fair. He took his salary, but nothing else beside. When his wife's car was booked in for a service, he insisted on paying for it in full (*very* unusual in the motor trade); if a friend purchased a car from the company they would get no greater discount than would be available to a regular and good customer and he would take none of the 'perks' that many directors considered to be theirs by right. He had no favourites. I remember at one time one of his closest friends came to work for the company, an individual he knew very well socially and liked a good deal. This person was treated exactly the same as any other member of staff and was criticised just as strongly when he failed to match up to the required standards. He was a tough wage-bargainer, but would pay what was necessary. He did not, it must be confessed, have any real commitment to employees sharing in the company's success beyond a fairly low level, but would reward competence and enthusiasm. This managing director had not got any degrees nor formal management qualifications and had no training, but he was one of the best and most respected managing directors I have known, because he was dedicated, honest and fair. To be sure, he had his blind spots — he found it difficult to have a good word to say for car salesmen — but this, he would claim, was not a blind spot but was fully justified by years of experience!

An honest and fair manager does not have to be a weak one. It is rarely possible to run a successful business without qualities of commitment and toughness. However, fairness and toughness need not be incompatible. Commitment can also be a moral quality — particularly from directors. When times are difficult it may be necessary to fight, and fight hard, to keep a business going. This can involve working seven days a week and can, sometimes, involve moral compromise. Unless directors are committed, the jobs of many employees may be lost and many lives adversely affected.

Morality can sometimes be a luxury. If the company has its back to the wall and survival is in serious question, then the directors may have to face a choice between high moral principles and going under. Moral compromise may be needed and this is not an easy area to deal with honestly. It is much easier to ignore it and assume that such situations do not arise — but anyone with extensive experience of the business world will know that they do.

I have in my time 'adjusted' figures submitted to banks who trusted me; deceived customers and creditors and been less than honest with colleagues. I have often been (as Sir William Armstrong, the former cabinet Secretary, admitted in court in Australia in 1987) 'economical with the truth' — albeit for reasons that seemed to be justifiable, as applied in the case of Sir William. I am not proud of any of these episodes, but think that I would do the same again if faced by similar situations. In all these cases, to the best of my recollection, I did not receive any direct personal benefit. There was a balance of moral responsibilities to be taken into account — there was no clear-cut 'right' answer.

I remember taking over responsibility for an engineering company in the north east of England. It employed about thirty-five people and had a history of losses. The company was on the verge of going under. Its net asset value (assets less liabilities) was only marginally positive and if a realistic view had been taken of the assets, then the value would have been negative. The bank was very sceptical about continuing support and, at the time of taking it over, was threatening a receiver. A budget was prepared for the year ahead based on reasonable sales expectations and these showed loses continuing and a cash-flow crisis. If these figures had been shown to the bank, a receiver would have been appointed the next day.

I had a number of choices available:

(1) To disclose the figures to the bank and accept the failure of the company.

(2) To disclose the figures to the bank but ask them to let us continue. In the circumstances, the chances of any reasonable person, let alone a banker, agreeing to this was slight. The bank had made clear its views — to protect itself it wished to appoint a receiver. I could not offer any promises as to the future nor any new ideas — I had none, beyond recruiting a new MD!

(3) To provide a guarantee to the bank from other

companies that I represented — but there was no
financial justification for doing this. The bank were
already at risk and if another company had given a
guarantee the risk would have been transferred to them
for no obvious benefit.

(4) To 'doctor' the forecast figures so that they reflected
greater optimism than the facts justified — particularly
by anticipating higher sales figures than seemed likely at
the time and anticipating lower costs, with no clear basis
for doing so. The bank would require some explanation
for this projected improvement, but reasons could be
thought up, even though they were based more on hope
than fact.

I chose the latter and, because I had a good record with
the bank, they agreed to give the company six months
grace — but to monitor the monthly figures carefully. A
new managing director was appointed although this took
several months. In the meantime the actual monthly figures
were turning out worse than the original budget. I altered
the accounting policies of the company, without telling the
bank, in order to reduce depreciation and reversed some of
the previous year-end stock write-downs — thus increasing
profit sufficiently to be in line with the forecast figures. The
bank had only the monthly figures to work on and these
looked reasonable.

The new managing director was, in fact, a success and
his efforts turned the company around. I had been told by a
previous director, 'The workers up here in the North East
are a lazy lot — they don't work like they do down South'. I
had repeated this to the new MD and his first action on
taking over was to call the whole workforce together,
explain in detail the situation the company faced and he
then passed on the comment I had relaid to him. The anger
of the northerners can be imagined! However this consultation had the desired effect and the new MD had the
employees putting their maximum effort into turning the

company round, improving quality and delivery dates and aggressively seeking new business.

I had deceived the bank and am not proud of doing so — but was this morally acceptable? Strictly speaking, it was not. I was less than honest with bankers who trusted me, and I had 'doctored' budgets and monthly figures (even though they were provisional and not audited and I had some basis for doing so). All turned out well in the end — but it might not have done.

In this situation the directors may have to weigh up their commitment to the company and the workforce against their duty to the bank and ask themselves in which direction true integrity lies. Only they can then decide, but if they took our principle seriously that 'people matter' and they recognised a duty to their employees, then it might be difficult for an outsider to condemn them. It is all too easy to see matters in black and white terms, until the time comes when the individual is faced by the real life problem.

Nevil Shute wrote a novel illustrating this dilemma called *Ruined City* in which a senior merchant banker placed his entire career and reputation on the line in order to bring work to a town in despair in the depression. He had to take part in shady practices in order to achieve his objective, including bribing foreign officials and raising money based on his considerable reputation, even though he was fairly sure that a financial disaster was likely, but he considered these to be prices that were worth paying. He ended up financially ruined and in gaol, but the shipyard on which the town depended was back on its feet and the town's men were working again. The novel forces consideration of the question whether this was or was not morally acceptable behaviour.

It is important to draw a distinction between directors who comprise moral standards for personal gain or to preserve their position and those who do so for some higher moral reason. Moral dilemmas *are* dilemmas — whether the field is abortion, nuclear weapons, divorce, research on embryos or in the business field. There are no simple rules — the director must balance the different moral demands, make his or her own decision and then abide by the consequences.

It would, of course, be too easy to say that duties to employees or the people one knows must take precedence over duties to institutions such as banks and insurance companies. However, straightforwardly at least, this position must be false and tensions such as those set out above cannot be so quickly resolved. Banks and insurance companies are themselves owned by individuals who often depend on them for pensions or their income. They may appear impersonal goliaths, but they cannot simply be looked on in this light.

Summary
The directors have a duty to shareholders to increase both profits and the asset value of the company, but they also need to establish its aims and direction. They need to take seriously their responsibilities to their employees who should matter to them as individuals and who, specifically, should not be simply treated as means to the end of profit. It is not good enough to dispense with the services of employees when they are no longer required — as if the company was disposing of an old piece of machinery.

Directors and managers should consider the development of an 'open' management style, involving managers and employees in the company's aims and objectives. Each employee should have objectives set for him or her each year and these should be frankly discussed with the individual by the manager. A written report setting out the objectives and how these have been fulfilled should be included in the employee's personal file. The company should not operate on a 'need to know' basis, but should give employees as much information as possible about the company's plans and intentions — thereby involving them in the company's future.

The Director and the Manager

Managers and directors have a moral responsibility, as well as an incentive in terms of increased efficiency, to train their employees to enable them to fulfil their potential as fully as possible. In order to do this, the company must be successful — it must be able to sell its goods or services at a profit in an increasingly competitive marketplace.

All employees of the company, from chairman to office cleaner, should be entitled to share in the fruits of success. Specifically the directors have no moral right to pay themselves substantial sums because of their unchallenged position of control within the company. Such a position is selfish and has no moral basis.

The directors are running the company for the shareholders but their moral obligations are not confined to the shareholders. Moral dilemmas are likely in which hard choices may have to be made which are not amenable to easy solutions.

Chapter Eight

THE COMPANY
AND THE CUSTOMER

World advertising is dominated by Western companies. The people that appear in jet-set situations, the smart and trendy people of the world are affluent, Western and white. It is not surprising, therefore, that those with black skins wish to emulate them. Mostly (with the exception of the US) those with black skin come from poor countries where there are few luxury goods. The number of cars, televisions, stereo sets, refrigerators and similar consumer durables per head of the population is markedly lower than in Western countries. For most people living in poorer countries, these durable goods remain out of reach — yet there are ways that these people can emulate the stars of the advertisements. In particular, they can make themselves look 'smarter' and 'more attractive' by lightening the colour of their skin.

Many British and American companies manufacture skin lightening creams and promote these actively. The implication of their advertising campaigns is that 'the smart set' are those with lighter skins. So powerful are these advertisements, that in many African countries women with lighter skin are considered to be the most attractive. Advertisements always portray the most beautiful girls as those with light skins and the population as a whole are influenced by this. Men, also, are considered to be more handsome if they have light skins. There are strong parallels in the Western world with tobacco companies seeking to promote the image of smoking cigarettes being the 'smart and trendy' thing for young people to emulate or with breweries promoting alcohol.

Financial and other companies with staff who have a high customer contact, sometimes seek to recruit employees who have lighter skin — by so doing, they give a more upmarket image of themselves.

In order to lighten black skins, creams, soaps or other cosmetics are used which sometimes contain mercury. The percentage of mercury in the product varies. Mercury can cause toxicity, it can poison and damage the skin. Prolonged use can cause the skin to go lumpy and the damage is permanent and irreversible. The pigmentation increases and creams are needed to soothe the skin and to hide the damage that has been caused. The cosmetics companies that manufacture the skin lightening creams also manufacture the products that are used to conceal the damage done.

In Britain, it is illegal to sell cosmetic products with more than two per cent mercury content. However some British companies have manufactured soaps and creams with concentrations as high as four or five per cent. These products may then be sold in the Third World at very high profit rates.

The remould tyre industry in Britain is a very large one. Lorries go round to tyre dealers and pick up the old tyres. The tyre dealers are generally not paid — they are glad to get rid of the huge stack of tyres they accumulate — although some remould companies do pay for worn out tyres, particularly of tyre sizes that are in short supply. The old tyres are then remoulded with new rubber being added and a new tread cut. It is a skilled operation and profit margins are slim. Much depends on a large volume of business and small remould manufacturers are rarely profitable. It is inevitable that some of the remould tyres have to be rejected as they fail to meet the stringent safety standards imposed for use on British roads. If a faulty tyre was sold in Britain and an accident happened as a result, the claim for compensation against the company could be very large indeed. The reject tyres cannot, therefore, be sold in this country. However considerable costs have been incurred on the reject tyres. Expensive rubber has been added to the old tyre and the labour involved in applying the tread pattern all has to be paid for.

Some remould manufacturers have therefore sold remould tyres which have been rejected for use in the British market to Third World countries where safety standards are low.

* * *

In Britain and America there are strict rules governing the sale of many products. There are 'trading standards officers' in Britain to ensure that goods sold are genuine and are of a 'merchantable quality'. They must be 'reasonably fit for the purpose for which they are intended'. Failure to abide by the laid-down standards can and does result in prosecution. The Advertising Standards Authority monitors advertisements and itself advertises asking members of the public to draw to its attention to suspect advertisements in order to ensure that they are legal, decent, honest and fair. The authority has considerable teeth. If it bans an advertisement, no UK radio, TV station, newspaper or magazine will handle it.

In spite of the above, moral questions do arise between a company and its customer. Certainly a company has an obligation, not only legal but from a moral as well as a prudent business point of view, to supply goods or services that live up to the description given and which fairly perform the function intended but it is not really in this area that the dilemmas arise.

Greater difficulties occur when companies may be tempted to supply goods which may be legal but which may do real damage to the customer. The tobacco industry is a good case in point. There is now little question that cigarettes damage health. They can lead to lung cancer, heart disease and cancer of the cervix in women. If pregnant mothers smoke, the children they are carrying may well be permanently damaged.

It may be argued that, in a free society, each individual should be able to make decisions for him or herself. If someone wants to rock climb, parachute, ski or smoke cigarettes they should be allowed to do so even though all these occupations carry risks. One cannot wrap free individuals in cotton wool. To do so would prevent them enjoying many of the pleasures of life.

This is a strong argument — although it is interesting that society specifically does not take this line when it comes to drugs. Drug taking and drug dealing are widely condemned, even though the taking of drugs is not restricted to the margins of society. One of the biggest groups of people using cocaine in recent years has been high-flyers in the cities of London and New York who have found that the 'charge' that cocaine gives helps them to perform well under stress at their offices. Cocaine, heroin, speed, smack and similar drugs are, it is true, highly addictive — but then so is tobacco. Indeed it can be argued that marijuana is less harmful and less addictive than tobacco (although there is always the danger that marijuana may lead onto the so-called 'hard' drugs). No-one, however, argues that the freedom of the individual should allow them to use cocaine if they so wish — use and possession of the drug is a serious criminal offence. Anyone supplying cocaine to others is prosecuted and faces an automatic and long prison term. Tobacco companies, on the other hand, are well regarded and are part of the 'establishment'.

Is it, then, morally acceptable to supply tobacco products? Given the government warnings on every packet of cigarettes and the fact that people are clearly aware of the dangers, it might well be held to be unreasonable to stop existing smokers buying cigarettes. Much more questionable, however, must be the advertising and promotion of cigarettes to young people. Because tobacco is partly addictive, if young people can be made to start smoking in their teenage years, they may well continue to smoke for much of their lives — thus providing the tobacco companies with an assured income. It is a fact of life that, although cigarettes are banned at most schools, they are regarded as a status symbol by many children. The children feel that they are 'with it' and grown up if they smoke and, therefore, they may smoke after school, in the toilets or behind the cricket pavilion. The promotion of cigarettes to such groups must be morally questionable.

Tobacco companies are, however, big employers. They buy tobacco from countries that are fairly poor and this helps the economy of these countries. They pay huge amounts in taxes and these funds can be used by the government to benefit the community. What is more, many people have money invested in these tobacco companies and depend on the income from them for pensions and savings. The tobacco companies have, for the last fifteen years, been trying as hard as possible to diversify — to reduce their dependence on tobacco profits. The question that such companies need to ask is whether they should accept any moral responsibility for promoting a product that is widely accepted to cause early death.

A similar problem arises for that most respectable group of British and American companies — the major clearing banks. National Westminster, Barclays, Lloyds, Midland as well as the smaller UK banks all participate in either the VISA or ACCESS credit cards, similarly US banks issue VISA or Master Charge cards. These are very profitable. When a customer at a shop, restaurant or garage presents one of these credit cards, the retailer loses between three and six per cent which is deducted from the amount of the sale by the credit card company. Provided the bill is paid by the customer in full within about three weeks of the statement, then the customer does not pay any charges at all. However payment does not need to be made in full — instead a small percentage of the total bill can be paid with the remainder left outstanding. This process can continue provided only that the individual's credit limit is not exceeded.

My wife has a VISA card and she regularly receives literature offering her loans. One missive was headed boldly 'MRS VARDY — £7500 IS READY AND AVAILABLE FOR YOU IN RETURN FOR JUST ONE 'PHONE CALL'. Now £7500 is a lot of money and many people may find this offer really attractive, but money borrowed must be repaid and the cost of borrowing can be horrendous.

The interest rates charged by the credit card companies are very high. Interest varies between 20 and 30 per cent per year. This means that, if an average of £1000 is owed to the credit card company during the year, an additional amount of interest of up to £300 has to be paid.

Credit cards are freely available and are actively promoted. Most people in Britain and the US have at least one and often more. The card companies encourage individuals to spend money that they may well not have and to 'spread their payments'. Although the interest rate is mentioned as a figure, many ordinary people are simply too naive to appreciate what this means. The result is that many of the poorest members of our society buy goods that they may well consider as necessities, using their credit cards. They soon run up total indebtedness at or very near to their credit limit. What is more, provided the minimum monthly payments are made, the credit card companies will regularly increase this credit limit.

If a young single mother, who may once have had a job and who therefore obtained credit cards, has both a VISA and an ACCESS card, both with credit limits of £1200 ($2000), she may easily have a total of £2000 ($3600) outstanding at any time to the credit card company. On this figure, she will have to pay interest to the card company of between £40 and £50 per month or about £10 per week. She simply cannot afford to do this. If she does not pay, however, the credit card company puts her under more and more pressure, even though she may be living on social security and may find it very difficult to make ends meet. This pressure may force her to go to moneylenders to clear off her borrowings (and it is likely that her debts will extend beyond the main credit card companies — she may well run up debts on store cards as well). Many firms offer loans to enable people in difficulties to clear off all their debts, but these loans will generally be secured on the house the person lives in, so if the individual defaults her house and possessions may be lost.

The result, therefore, of banks promoting credit cards may be that families in need end up homeless.

Here we have a clear moral problem. The banks behave perfectly properly and according to the law in advertising their rates of interest. They also make some attempt to assess spending limits. It is, they may argue, up to the customer to decide whether he or she can afford the payments. A person, they may say, must take responsibility for his or her own actions. This is reasonable enough, but the question arises whether a company has a responsibility to customers who may not be particularly intelligent; who may fall on hard times or who may find the encouragement to 'spend now' difficult to resist. The parallels between banks and tobacco companies are very close.

The directors and managers who run banks and building societies are, of course, highly intelligent individuals — they are perfectly capable of deciding for themselves whether or not to smoke or to borrow. I would, in fact, strongly suspect that no such managers or directors ever borrow on their credit card as this form of credit is very expensive. It will always be much cheaper for those who are credit-worthy to borrow from their banks on overdraft. An overdraft may cost little more than half the interest rate applied by the banks on credit card borrowing. This is why, of course, banks find credit card business so very profitable. What this does mean is that the people who borrow on credit cards are those who are least credit worthy and least able to afford to get into difficulties. Most credit card customers do operate their accounts properly and without getting into difficulties — the problem comes with those who do not.

Can the general principle we formulated in earlier chapters help us in this situation? Clearly credit cards are very useful and helpful. No-one could reasonably suggest they should be done away with or that credit facilities should be abandoned. If, however, customers are to be treated as individuals who really matter, whose interests must be taken into account, then questions need to be asked as to how these interests are best safeguarded. As so often in the business field, this is not a simple matter. At the least, however, there is a case for credit card companies reassessing their attitude to customers who continually run high levels of indebtedness. For instance by:

1. Not automatically increasing credit facilities to any customer who has not cleared his account at any time in the last six months. This would avoid constant increases of credit to customers who may not be in a position to finance the payments. Such customers could still request increases in their credit limit if they so wished, but they themselves would have to take the initiative.

2. Restricting credit to those living on social security benefits alone or who do not clearly have the means to pay.

3. Sending out specific letters explaining the costs of borrowing and the dangers of running too high balances on credit card accounts. This, of course, would demand considerable moral courage from the directors as it would run against normal marketing policy. It would mean warning potential customers of the dangers they face and this might deter customers from further borrowing. This would face the directors with the decision as to whether people or profits come first.

4. Devoting much greater efforts to helping and assisting those who get into difficulties as a result of debts to credit card companies. This would mean these companies allocating a greater percentage of their very considerable

profits to payment of advisers who would help and assist customers when they had difficulties. These advisers could have available to them the whole range of services which are available from the banks who operate the credit cards and which might be used to help to refinance the debt in a manageable way.

If, therefore, there is a substantial backlog of payments or a solid core of borrowing which the customer cannot reduce, the bank might review all the circumstances and, possibly, provide a second mortgage at a reasonable rate of interest to clear the balance. Instead, therefore, of a woman having £3000 outstanding on various credit cards at an interest rate of 28 per cent, a second mortgage could be provided to clear this indebtedness at an interest rate of 14 per cent and with repayments spread over ten years or more. This would avoid pushing the woman into the hands of dubious financiers and would retain the moral integrity of the credit card companies. Such an attitude would, of course, be expensive as the companies would have to take some responsibility for helping their customers rather than just treating them as 'bad payers' who must be hounded until payment is made. However this is precisely the attitude that banks take to Third World countries who cannot repay their debts, so in principle at least there seems no reason why a similar approach could not be taken to bank customers. Indeed banks have already made provisions of in excess of 30 per cent against many Third World loans, so it is not only personal bad debts that can be costly!

The problem would be more difficult if the woman could not offer property as security, but the problem still has to be faced and it should be treated as a joint problem of *both* the credit card company *and* the customer — not simply a matter for the customer to suffer through alone and unaided.

The moral issue of whether a company has a responsibility for its customers in relation to products and services supplied is a clear one. It simply will not do to say that people have been informed and must take responsibility for their own actions. This does not work in the case of drugs and many people do not have the personal resources to cope with too great temptations deliberately placed in their way.

The British and US stock markets are currently standing at high levels. The 1980s have seen one of the longest stock market booms in history with the exception of the massive fall in October 1987 — although even this did not do more than mark a reduction in the height of the boom. Always in the past, however, there has been a bear market after a bull — in other words past history points ahead to a future fall in stock market values. Perhaps, of course, past history is no guide and, defying the law of gravity, stock prices around the world will move inexorably upwards. However, it is as well to remember Churchill's words:

'He who will not learn from history is compelled to repeat it.'

Still, however, unit trust managers, pension funds and financial advisers point to the advisability of investing in stock markets around the world. The Unit Trust industry has its own regulatory body now, *Lautro*, and this has some teeth. When Marks and Spencer were going to introduce their own unit trusts to be promoted in their shops, they printed the promotional material but were then told by *Lautro* that they were in breach of its rules. *Lautro* requires Unit Trust promotion material to contain a warning that the capital value and income from the trust can fluctuate. Further, the wording must not contain a sub-clause that would 'disguise the significance' of this warning. The M&S original form said:

Although the prices of units can go down as well as up, unit trusts are one of the soundest long-term investments.

It was the latter clause that troubled *Lautro*.

The question arises whether this warning, even without the sub-clause, is enough. Certainly unit trusts *have been* one of the soundest long-term investments, but this does not mean they will continue to be so. The US's federal deficit is still at quite incredible levels (about $150 000 million per year), and increased interest rates are imposing yet further strains on Third World countries — with consequent risks of failures in the Western banking system and with real dangers of major currency realignments. Given that fund managers are dealing with money invested with them by people who may be relying on their skill for their retirement income, there are moral questions to be faced as to how this money should be invested. Should the fund manager go all out for growth in order to ensure that his company is at the top of the performance league tables or, rather, learning from history should a more prudent approach be required? As we have seen so often, there is no clear right or wrong answer.

At the least pension funds and others handling investors funds should make their customers aware of the dangers as well as the opportunities and should seek to explain the risks. If this is done, no blame can be attached if markets fall and many people lose a great deal of money. If, however, salesmen and advertisements hold out only the promise of rising returns, then a heavy responsibility will lie on the managers and those responsible for promotion when the collapse comes. Midland Bank, in promoting their Meridian range of unit trusts, gave an example of real openness and honesty, when they said the following in their promotion literature:

> As with any investment in stocks and shares it is possible that the value of your holding may fall below the amount originally invested as the price of units, and the income from them, can go down as well as up.
>
> Because they are dependent on the performance of the companies in which they invest, Unit Trusts carry some

risk. This risk is made up of two elements: that individual companies may perform badly, or the whole stockmarket may go into reverse.

One of the golden investment rules is to avoid putting all your eggs into one basket. Investing in Unit Trusts does just this and reduces the risk of poor individual performance by investing in a broad spectrum of companies. And the key to successful investment lies in riding out occasional stockmarket reverses. So we recommend that you should not commit funds that you do not have plans to spend within the next three years or so. So, yes, there is an element of risk, but there is also the potential for substantial growth in the future.

No company could put the position more clearly or fairly than this. Sadly, such openness is not always a common feature of those promoting investments. High, undisclosed commission payments and management charges have been a feature of the field as have wildly optimistic forecasts of future performance. This is one reason why it has been necessary to introduce FIMBRA — the association of independent financial advisers. Members of this body have to meet certain laid-down disclosure and ethical standards and the aim is to avoid some of the abuses that have occurred in the investment field in the past.

The issues raised by the two examples at the beginning of this chapter (skin lightening products and remould tyres) seem easier to deal with as they are more clear cut. By any standard, supplying a product to an overseas country which will cause disease and disfigurement must be wrong. Still more is this so if the product is actively promoted. There is no reason why a black skin is any less or more beautiful than a white or yellow one. Beauty, after all, is in the eye of the beholder. To actually educate people, through the highly persuasive and subtle use of advertising, that light skins are more attractive than dark, is not only blatant commercial exploitation with the aim of profit but, more to the point, diminishes the humanity and feeling of human worth of those people with dark skins who see the advertisements. It is almost worse than apartheid, as it is persuading people with a certain colour skin that they are inherently less worthy of respect and status than others whose skin tone is different.

A similar problem occurred ten years ago with the active promotion of powdered baby milk in Third World countries. Huge posters were put up and colour advertisements inserted in newspapers and magazines showing happy, well fed babies and implying that this was the result of using powdered milk. The result was thousands of deaths. Instead of breast feeding, many women started to use powdered milk. They could not, however, afford the proper quantities so they diluted the powder so much that the babies were malnourished. Also, the water they used to make up the milk was frequently dirty and carried disease — not due to the mothers' fault, but because clean water was not available and the women were not aware of the dangers. Babies died as a result. By depriving them of the breast, the babies were also deprived of the mother's antibodies which provided protection against many local diseases.

The issue of remould tyres is a more difficult one. Many Third World countries desperately need transport. They often have vehicles, but cannot afford spare parts. To be able to buy tyres at a low price means that transport is possible whereas, if the full price had to be paid for perfect tyres, very few could be imported. It could be argued that the lower quality though less safe tyre is better than no tyre at all. The issue is not straightforward and a difficult judgement would have to be made as to just how safe or unsafe the rejected tyres really are.

One way of facing the issue is for the directors or those responsible to ask themselves whether they could seriously face the people who have suffered as a result of their products. Would the chairman of a company making mercury-based skin lightening creams be happy to meet and see the effects his company's products have had on a beautiful young black girl's skin? Would he be content to know that she had been marked for life and rejected, perhaps, by her husband as a result? Would the director of the tyre remould company be happy to meet the widow of the man killed by the defective tyre and to explain to her that his life was the price that necessarily had to be paid in order that his country could achieve a higher standard of mobility? Would the directors of the large banks be willing to meet the young mothers made homeless by debt?

Too often directors and managers insulate themselves in their cocooned offices and comfortable houses from the results of their decisions and refuse to really look at the possible consequences. If the importance of moral decisions are to be taken seriously, and not avoided, then the least that any of us can do is TO LOOK AT THE POTENTIAL RESULTS OF OUR ACTIONS ON CUSTOMERS AND TO ASK OURSELVES WHETHER WE ARE WILLING TO LIVE WITH THESE CONSEQUENCES. A refusal to look, a refusal to examine and review is a refusal to face up to the moral demand. This is, in fact, quite a good test to apply in any moral dilemma. If we genuinely ask ourselves whether we are prepared to live with the consequences of decisions we make, we can tell ourselves a good deal about whether these actions are or are not appropriate.

Some products are, in themselves, morally neutral but it is the use to which they are put that may be questionable. Land-Rover still makes one of the best four-wheeled-drive vehicles in the world. They are exported to many countries and do sterling service in keeping communication links open, in helping doctors and nurses to get through in dreadful conditions, in enabling farmers to work land that would otherwise be inaccessible, and generally to assist in Third World development. However anyone who has seen the film *Cry Freedom* will have seen that the South African police are equipped with Land-Rovers and, some would hold, these police are the instruments of a brutal and repressive regime. Is it, then, wrong to sell Land-Rovers to South Africa?

This issue is far from clear cut. The South African police are certainly not all bad. They are efficient and come rapidly to the help of many in trouble. When the 'necklace killings' were taking place in Soweto, when faction fights break out between tribal groups on the mines, when burglaries or riots occur the police are there to try to restore order or to catch those responsible. To be sure, they can also sometimes be brutal and often prefer the protection of white people to the legal interests of the black community. It really does not seem to be easily possible for the management of Land-Rover to make a moral decision in these circumstances. For Land-Rover to say, 'We will only sell our vehicles to governments who are never repressive' would mean that they might have no sales at all — after all, even the British government has on occasion been condemned by Amnesty International over its treatment of some prisoners in Northern Ireland.

The businessman or woman cannot, realistically, be expected to be the conscience of the world. He or she cannot hope or attempt to resolve all the moral problems of a fragmented world in which moral standards may well vary. Certainly responsibility must be taken for the products supplied and for consequences that flow directly from their use, but it does seem unreasonable to expect a great deal more. It is hard enough to run a profitable business in the face of intense domestic and international competition; it is even harder to behave properly to one's own employees. Some responsibility must be accepted for products a firm manufactures but morality can also be a luxury. There must be limits to the range of possibilities that a firm can reasonably be expected to consider. Pragmatism may not be the best of moral principles, but no one can run a business in the real world without a touch of pragmatism.

The above paragraph is, however, somewhat obscure. What are 'consequences that flow directly from a product's use'? An arms manufacture knows that, if his weapons are used, they will cause death, suffering and destruction. However he will also know that strong defences in the West have kept the peace in Europe for more than 44 years. A strong defence industry can thus be held to contribute to peace. Perhaps a Quaker, who never believes in fighting under any circumstances, even if he or she is attacked, might reject arms manufacture. For anyone else to do so, it would be difficult to reject such manufacture just because the weapons might be used by a legitimate government. What *might*, however, legitimately be rejected would be the direct or indirect supply to terrorist organisations which would use them to destroy civilians.

The marginal areas occur where repressive regimes use arms *either* to repress their local population *or* to take up arms against their neighbour for expansionist or ideological reasons. Of course, the situation may not always be clear cut and an arms manufacturer may well not have a tender conscience. Much may also depend on the manufacturer's own presuppositions. A Western manufacturer would probably be happy to supply arms to a government resisting communist incursions, whereas a communist manufacturer certainly would not. However the one point that is clearly wrong would be to supply arms to anyone, anywhere, in any circumstances, provided only that they can pay. One person's terrorist is another person's freedom fighter. At the least, some moral deliberation is appropriate.

Summary

Any company manufacturing a product which will knowingly inflict harm or cause distress to customers, even if the customers' attention is drawn to this, needs to consider whether it is in a defensible moral position. At the least, managers and directors should be willing to personally face up to the consequences of what they are doing and not to hide away from the probable results of their actions. They should be guided by the principle that 'people matter' and this applies whether it is an American or a British consumer or even a peasant and her children living in desperately poor conditions in the Third World. The moral demand of care and concern for the consequences of the use of products goes beyond the straightforward legal boundaries and rests clearly on our initial principle — that every human being is important.

Having said this, a director cannot be expected to be the conscience of the world and it is unrealistic to expect, except in exceptional circumstances, that a firm must refuse to supply products unless the final end uses to which they might be put are first carefully verified. An inherently sound and good product, therefore, can be abused and this is not the company's fault. Rat poison could be used to poison my wife, but the latter act could hardly be blamed on the manufacturers of the poison!

Chapter Nine

THE COMPANY
AND THE SUPPLIER

John was a plumber and Bill was a carpenter and mason. They were both made redundant from a firm of Yorkshire house builders and decided to set up in business together to act as general builders. They were bored with taking orders, often from foremen who were less skilled than them, and were confident in their own abilities. They both had their own tools and John had a one-ton Ford pick-up truck which they decided to use for their new business. They started in a small way and orders started to come in immediately. There was no problem getting work and, once the work started, more came in from recommendations from their customers.

The business built up steadily and, at the end of six months, the two partners had taken on a skilled electrician and two YTS assistants. Bill's wife, Lisa, looked after the books and accounts. The jobs the new firm handled gradually became larger and the end of the first year saw them renovating houses for small development companies. Cash flow pressures were, however, building up. Customers owed them a considerable sum of money and they had a large overdraft, secured on their houses. When everyone paid them, they would make a considerable profit but in the meantime the bank was applying some pressure.

Then two disasters struck. The partners had carried out a £7000 renovation job on a local sales manager's house. His wife ran off with her hairdresser and the husband queried the bill for the renovation work and refused to pay — saying that he was not happy with some of the work and that his wife was responsible for most of the bill. Then a development company which had given the new firm a contract to split a house into two flats announced that it had run into financial problems because of the slowing down of the property market and would have to delay payment for work done until the flats were sold. The bank refused to increase the partners' overdraft any further and suppliers pressed hard for payment — refusing to supply any more goods until their accounts were cleared in full. This brought further work to a halt.

John and Bill's firm went into liquidation and both of them had to sell their houses to pay their debts. Four out of five new businesses in Britain similarly fail within five years — generally from cash-flow problems.

* * *

In the above case, the infant firm was largely dependent on its suppliers. The suppliers were much larger than the new firm and could insist that their laid-down credit terms were met. The ultimate sanction was the cessation of all supplies and liquidation soon followed. Of course, the firm had a moral obligation to pay its suppliers but its inability to do this owed more to poor financial controls and lack of adequate working capital than to any act of will by the partners.

The situation is, however, rather different when the roles are reversed and a small company is the supplier whilst a large company is the customer. Small companies are usually hungry for business and will normally be only too pleased if they obtain orders, often substantial in relation to their size, from a big concern. Such orders may be very important indeed in the early stages and the turnover they represent may be a significant proportion of the young firm's total business. However the relationship is unequal and this lack of equality is sometimes exploited by the larger firm. The exploitation can be achieved in various ways.

The Company and the Supplier

1. Perhaps most common, is for the larger firm to delay payments for goods and services supplied until well after the normal date for payment. There is little or nothing the smaller firm can do about this — a small firm cannot easily take a huge company to court and any threat to withhold supplies may cut off the major source of business. It will harm the small firm more than the large one. From the large firm's viewpoint, the longer the company can delay paying its bills, the more profitable it will become. A small example will illustrate this.

Imagine a company distributes and sells sporting goods. For the sake of simplicity, let us assume that they only deal in baseballs. They buy in the baseballs from various small suppliers at $5 per ball. They buy in and sell 10000 baseballs a month. They keep one month's stock in their shops and warehouses. They sell the balls at $8 each and their customers pay them, on average, 60 days after delivery so at any time there are two months' sales of baseballs outstanding. The Working Capital section of the Balance Sheet would be as follows:

CURRENT ASSETS		
Stock of baseballs (10000 × $5)		50000
Debtors (20000 × $8)		160000
		210000
CURRENT LIABILITIES		
Amount owing to suppliers. One month's supply (10000 × $5)		50000
INVESTMENT REQUIRED IN WORKING CAPITAL		$160000

A new managing director comes in, determined to increase profits. He cannot force customers to pay more quickly as then they might buy elsewhere, so he gives instructions to his accounts office that, instead of paying for goods delivered after one month, the company should forthwith delay payments for *four* months. Of course, this will make life difficult for the small baseball manufacturers who supply the company, but there are plenty of them and if they do not like the situation there is little they can do as there are few alternative outlets. The accounts office may be told to make excuses for non-payment but not to release any payments until four months have elapsed.

The Working Capital position of the company will now appear as follows:

CURRENT ASSETS (As above, no change) 210 000

CURRENT LIABILITIES
   Amount owing to suppliers
    Four month's supply (4 ×10 000 × $5)   200 000

INVESTMENTS REQUIRED
IN WORKING CAPITAL $ 10 000

The effect has been quite dramatic. The amount the company has to find in order to finance its working capital has been reduced from $160 000 to $10 000 — thus releasing $150 000. This would save a great deal of money on interest charges as well as generating cash that could be used elsewhere to expand the business. Both of these would contribute to increased profits. The cost, of course, has to be born by the small suppliers — many of whom may not be able to afford the considerable increase in cash resources that are required or the cost of the additional finance.

If the new managing director is really cynical, he may deliberately try to drive some of the small manufacturers out of business. He could then pick up their equipment from the liquidators at negligible cost and start a manufacturing operation of his own.

2. The larger firm may give the new, small supplier large orders initially. Payments may be made on time and the new firm cannot believe its good fortune. The large customer increases orders still further until the point is reached where something like 70 to 80 per cent of the small firm's business goes to the single customer. At this point, the large firm may move in with a gentle ultimatum, requiring the small supplier to either drop its prices substantially in future, or risk losing all its business — which it cannot now afford to do as it has geared itself up to a high level of production, or else to accept a low offer to buy the company out — again backed by the threat that if this is not accepted, orders will cease.

3. Many small firms start up because their owners have a bright new idea. A large firm may come in with substantial orders until it is thoroughly familiar with the new approach and all the technology involved and may then move to hire the key people from the small firm or, simply, set up its own competing operation to perform the same function — thus effectively depriving the small firm of its niche in the market.

Not all large firms behave like this, of course, but many certainly do. Any excuse may be good enough to delay payment. The large firm holds all the cards — and it knows it. Imagine a publicly quoted group of companies with debts outstanding to suppliers of £360 million and these represent, on average, sixty days worth of sales (about average for US and British industry). If payment can just be delayed by seven days, so that the average period of credit taken from suppliers rises from 60 to 67 days, then the amount owing to creditors will rise to £402 million. In other words, a seven-day delay in payment will generate an additional £42 million of cash resources that do not have to be paid for (the larger the amount owing to creditors, the less finance a firm needs!). Small wonder that many large firms delay payments as long as they can.

Not all companies tell their suppliers officially that they are going to delay payment. In some companies (perhaps 'many companies' would be more accurate) the company accountant 'juggles' creditor payments continually to keep the company within its laid-down overdraft limit. Some of the best company accountants I have known, certainly in medium-sized companies, have had their working lives dominated by cash-flow management. Every day they have to balance the previous day's bank balance against what is coming in and what has to go out. The accounts department may well draw all the cheques for suppliers, but some accountants retain the larger cheques in their draw — only releasing them when the need arises. By so doing, they maintain a tight control on their cash-flow position and, of course, the longer they can delay sending out the cheques the longer they have the supplier's cash to use in their own company. Some of the excuses commonly used by firms to delay payments to suppliers include:

(a) Sorry, one of the cheque signatories is on holiday for two weeks. We'll send you the cheque when he returns.

(b) The cheque was put in the post yesterday. (This may well not be true, but when the supplier has waited for the cheque that does not arrive, a new one has to be drawn and the old one cancelled, thus delaying payment).

(c) We have a query on your invoice. We have written to you. (A query on one small item of a large invoice can give an excuse for delaying payment of the whole amount whilst the 'dispute' is resolved).

(d) There has been a delay in approving some of the items due to holidays. We hope to overcome the backlog as soon as possible.

Whilst these devices are certainly understandable, they can hardly be regarded as moral. It is a matter of lying to suppliers, of breaching agreements as to payment terms, of exploiting the weakness of smaller firms — all in the interests of profit. Although our general principle does not

119

have direct application here, it seems clear that, by the standards it is trying to uphold, this can hardly be regarded as morally acceptable behaviour — although when a company is faced with the choice between doing this and going out of business (as was the case with John and Bill's building firm at the beginning of this chapter) it is, perhaps, an understandable route to take and directors or managers may have to weigh up moral priorities.

Some few companies have gone in exactly the opposite direction and have sought to develop, as a matter of policy, a really close working relationship with suppliers — and there can be much to be gained from this approach. Marks and Spencer were one of the first major companies to develop a close relationship with those companies that produced many of the clothes they sold. They stipulated exactly what their requirements were — both in terms of style and quality. Their representatives visited their suppliers' factories and, in return for guaranteed and substantial orders, monitored production and the quality of the goods supplied very closely indeed. M&S developed a close relationship with their suppliers and found tremendous benefits resulted — quality was improved, costs were kept down and the suppliers were assured that payments would be made regularly. Of course, the small supplier paid a price — it became highly dependent on M&S business and its profits were, effectively, controlled by M&S management and by the profits they 'permitted' (since, in the end, M&S would determine the price they were prepared to pay for goods and, thus, the profit margin the supplier would achieve).

Another technique used by large companies is to prevent competitors ever becoming suppliers — either to them or to their customers. IBM is the largest manufacturer of computers in the world. It has the biggest research and development programme and its products are usually in the forefront of technical design and innovation. IBM does, however, have a marketing problem. As soon as it produces a new machine, many smaller manufacturers will produce 'clones' — similar machines which can do as much as the new IBM but at a lower cost. IBM has had to incur the tremendous expense of developing brand new technology and, as soon as its machine is launched, all the competitors take the machine to pieces, make copies (with a few alterations and sometimes improvements) and then undercut the computer giant.

In recent years, IBM has found its market share slipping because of the manufacture of 'clones' and it has therefore sought to introduce a new disc operating system (DOS) for its personal computers. This is the system or 'language' in accordance with which the computer operates, which competitors will take time to copy. The new operating system is called OS/2 and this will gradually replace what has become the industry standard — MS/DOS IBM, however, faces at least two problems with the introduction of the new system:

(1) It is going to have to persuade its customers, all of whose systems presently work on MS/DOS, to change to OS/2. OS/2 is faster and a better system, but change is traumatic for companies and programmers and others will have to get used to the new thinking and develop new skills,

(2) In the United States there are 'anti-trust' laws which effectively prevent IBM cornering the market and which will force it to make the new system available to competitors.

It is difficult not to have some sympathy for IBM who has to be the pioneer and engage in enormous research and development expenditure — only to have its work taken up by leaner and more hungry competitors. Of course, IBM has many advantages — it has great buying power and can attempt to 'corner the market' in the latest microchips or tie up exclusive contracts with suppliers. This is all part of the jungle within which any business has to operate and

121

morality is scarcely an issue. Even taking an IBM machine to pieces and copying it can hardly be regarded as immoral — it should be a part of any company's normal policy to constantly examine and review the products of its competitors. Any company that ignores its competitors will soon find itself falling behind in the race for excellence and innovation. IBM, and similar large companies, have no alternative but to continue to keep ahead of the pack — by spending more on research and development and ensuring that their products are always at the forefront of technological development.

It is, of course, a different matter when industrial espionage is involved. At the 1988 Farnborough Air Show, one of the Western world's most advanced suppliers of 'look down' radar for fighter aircraft found that its stand had been broken into. This radar enables a fighter pilot to look below him and target his missiles at hostile aircraft or even at enemy positions on the ground. It is highly complex as it has to distinguish the targets from general 'ground clutter' and from moving objects such as cars. Nothing was stolen, but photographs of key pieces of equipment were taken. The firm did not know whether the espionage was undertaken by an Eastern bloc country (Czechoslovakia was suspected) or by another Western country or company anxious to obtain the secrets of the latest technology for its own use. Clearly the latter is unacceptable moral behaviour — yet, strangely, the same behaviour by the Russians may, from their point of view, be completely moral as it is all part of the process of 'defending the mother-land'. After all, if American spies seek to get access to Eastern bloc secrets, we in the West tend to consider their behaviour morally acceptable.

It may be more difficult if a supplier is asked to produce a product for a firm and then decides to make a copy and sell it under its own name. An engineering company of which I was a director won a contract to produce digging implements to fit on a range of small Japanese tractors. The designs were supplied and the product had been well thought out. We decided to copy the design, make small changes so that we did not infringe the Japanese company's copyright, and sell it at a lower price using our own brand name. Was this immoral? We were safeguarding the jobs of our workers as the company was in a vulnerable position. We did tell the Japanese company what we were doing just before we launched the product — we wanted, and managed, to keep their business as well! — but we would probably have been willing to go ahead even without their approval as we were sure that the demand for our lower price product would outstrip theirs. If, of course, we had been required to give an undertaking of secrecy, then breach of this undertaking would clearly have been immoral, but in the absence of such an undertaking it was a purely commercial decision for us to make as to whether it was worth producing our own design, even if this meant losing the Japanese company's business in the future.

Within Western countries, companies are free to decide where to place their orders. They will go to the firm that can produce the best quality compatible with low prices and reliable delivery. A supplier that fails to match up to the required standard will be replaced by another. Consistent failure to meet the standards required in the market place will inevitably result in failure. This is one reason why successful companies (for instance in the pharmaceutical, chemical, oil, motor vehicle, engineering, electronics and many other industries) are willing to invest such large amounts in research and development. They are striving to stay ahead of the competition, to develop the new product or process that will win orders.

The 'survival of the fittest' was, Darwin found, the mechanism whereby evolutionary forces produced changes in animals and plants to fit the species for changing conditions. The same mechanism is at work in a free market. Companies that are not efficient, that do not keep up to date with the latest developments will, inevitably, die to be replaced by more efficient methods, better products and more effective promotion and advertising. The striving for excellence in product design, product features, ease of use and lower costs, continually drives one company on to keep ahead of another.

This is one reason why protectionism behind trade barriers is such a mistake. The United States, at present, is faced by the temptation to turn protectionist — in other words to erect high tariff barriers to make it more difficult for foreign firms to sell in the US market. In the short term, these tariff barriers ensure a boom in trade for companies within the protected market. A parallel situation occurred when sanctions were applied against Rhodesia — foreign goods became difficult to obtain and local manufacturers enjoyed a boom as competition was stifled. Domestic companies immediately enjoy a price advantage in comparison with their competitors who have to sell over the tariff barrier. Protectionism is, however, a dangerous tool as it encourages complacency. Domestic firms are protected from international competition and are no longer forced to innovate and to remain in the forefront of technological developments and product design. The result is that the country's products become less and less attractive in world markets.

Britain found this in the late 1970s. Its industry was in decline and economic performance was dreadful. Some politicians proposed protectionism. Instead, at the beginning of the 1980s, the doors were thrown open making Britain a largely free market. The results were immediate — the 'old' industries nearly collapsed: profits fell or losses increased, workforces were heavily cut back and unemployment soared. By the end of the 80s, however, the benefits were being reaped with more and more new companies being formed which could compete in world markets and hold their own against any competition. A good example was the luxury car company, Jaguar.

The 1960s and 70s saw a mania for amalgamations in the

motor industry. By the end of the 1970s there was a single, inefficient British owned volume motor manufacturer — the British Leyland Motor Corporation. It had many factories and brand names, cars which were old fashioned and poorly made and it specialised in losses (in fact, British Leyland's auditor's refused to allow the company to treat the losses resulting from the closure of factories as 'extraordinary items' as the company was closing factories on such a regular basis that they held it was in the business of closing factories and the losses were not extraordinary!). The group survived by courtesy of massive government aid.

Jaguar was a part of this large group. The once proud name, synonymous with speed, luxury and quality, was now famous for inefficiency and the frequency with which the cars broke down. Sales were collapsing, particularly in the important US market. Many dealers were giving up the franchise and the price of second-hand Jaguars tumbled. A buyer of a new Mercedes-Benz could expect his car to depreciate by about 20 per cent in the first year — in the case of Jaguars the figure was in excess of 50 per cent.

Then plans were announced for Jaguar to be privatised. A new management team was brought in. The first thing that the new management did was to place a heavy emphasis on the quality of the product. Posters in the factory, meetings on the factory floor plus a campaign throughout the company emphasised the need for the highest quality and that the customer was king. New designs were produced and a major new promotion campaign began in the US. Jaguar was then 'floated off' as a separate public company with management and workers having a substantial share stake.

The results were a classic case of what can be achieved by good management. Quality improved dramatically (and quickly), customers realised what was happening and demand picked up — slowly at first, but with increased rapidity. The 'Jaguar' name was already a legend and, trading on this, the company promoted its new cars vigorously. Losses became rising profits, the second-hand value of Jaguar cars improved and the company entered and won the World Sports Car Championship and the Le Mans 24-Hour race — winning against the best competition in the world. Instead of a lame duck, a fledgling eagle emerged from the painful chrysallis of crisis and losses. It was, however, a fledgling that would continue to have to fight to survive in the toughest markets in the world — in the face of fierce competition from Mercedes-Benz, Porsche, BMW, Toyota, Honda and US manufacturers.

Capitalism is a hard task master and casualties are inevitable (causing great suffering — talk to the tens of thousands laid off in the steel and shipbuilding industries of Europe and America who, as they near retirement age, face the future with little hope of employment), but it rewards success. Exactly the same situation applies in the animal kingdom where the strongest and fittest survive and the weak die. Nature is also a hard taskmaster — it is 'red in tooth and claw'. The weakest animal in a litter or group is killed or fails to survive. The beautiful, doe-eyed gazelle is torn to pieces by the lion whilst her head is eaten by the vultures. Similarly the once-proud company that refuses to keep up to date and to adapt to changing conditions will die and its assets will be stripped by leaner and hungrier companies who will prosper on what they have plundered.

Neither nature nor capitalism is compassionate. Both reward success and both litter history with the corpses of failures. Both, however, succeed in their purposes. Nature uses the principle of natural selection to weed out the weak so that the strong will breed and survive. Similarly capitalism is always weeding out the weak.

Sometimes there may be a choice between a company giving an order either to a highly automated plant or to one which pays very low wages but uses many human workers. What may appear 'right' on the surface in this situation is not, however, always clear cut. An example will illustrate this.

Britain and the United States have a history of taking in refugees. These refugees often move, initially, into the poorest areas of large cities and, over the decades, by hard work and showing initiative they gradually 'better themselves' and move out to more prosperous areas.

Many people from South-East Asia came into Britain and the US after the fall of South Vietnam to the North Vietnamese. They were, of course, allowed to draw social security benefit but found it very difficult to live on this. Some could not speak English and jobs were hard to come by — particularly for women. The women had few skills, except that they were used to sewing. Small workshops were therefore established, in conditions almost reminiscent of Victorian 'sweat shops' where groups of women worked on sewing machines to 'make up' dresses and other clothes for smart West End and Fifth Avenue boutiques. The pay was dreadful — often less than £1 ($2) per hour.

Surely this amounts to exploitation? Are not the West End boutiques using these refugees who have no hope of any other jobs to produce garments at a very low cost and are, thus, exploiting them?

However the moral position is not as simple as first appears. These women often remain on social security although, of course, they should not, legally, do so as they have jobs. By combining the small income from social security with the even smaller amount they get by working on clothes, they have enough money for their families to enjoy a basic and sustainable standard of living. If they acted legally, they would not have enough to live on. If the boutiques were compelled to pay a proper wage rate for their garments, they would then go to one of the big firms with modern machinery who could produce the garments much more cheaply than if they were done by hand at a 'fair' rate — the refugees would then have no jobs at all.

Moral issues are not always simple, neither is the first reaction ('refugees exploited by West End boutiques' or 'Refugees break social security rules') necessarily the right one. Certainly the refugees *are* breaking the law and, if they were caught, they would be punished. This is a case where our general principle ('People matter . . .') may well have lessons to teach us which go against what may at first seem the obvious reaction. Before anyone condemns the refugees for 'earning a bit of money on the side', they should, perhaps, try living with small children in very poor conditions in a foreign country with scarcely enough money to pay the high rent that is charged for accommodation. Few of us have never broken the law. If we are motorists, how many can claim never to have broken the speed limit or parked on a yellow line? Before we rush to moral condemnation of those who, in need, earn a little extra money that they are not strictly entitled to, we should, perhaps, look to ourselves. Jesus put it nicely: 'Let him who is without sin cast the first stone'!

Those who put principles and rules first, before the importance of people, can sometimes be the hardest and coldest of all. They can be quick to judge others, quick to see the obviously right solution and quick to avoid discussion of the complexities.

Five American anti-apartheid groups issued the following statement in January 1987 to support their view that multinational companies should disinvest from South Africa:

> We support an end to all corporate involvement in or with South Africa and Namibia.

American companies came under heavy pressure to pull out of South Africa. The American subsidaries were good employers. Many of them operated an 'equal pay for equal work' policy. They refused to recognise the apartheid rules within their factories. They helped with the education of children of employees and ensured that medical care and pensions for workers and their families were at a high level. Their training schemes were good and they were not afraid of promoting black workers. However pressure in the US forced many American companies to disinvest from South Africa — 114 withdrew between 1986 and 1988.

General Motors was one of the best employers in South Africa but, because of pressure, they sold out their South African operation to local management who operate under the name Delta Motors. The sale took place on 31st December, 1986. Once they had done this, 'forced into complying with proper moral principles' as many put it, then Delta is alleged to have adopted a much tougher stand towards the unions. A NUMSA (the union involved) spokesman said that since the buyout:

> Management 'has really put the screws on' and it is now 'totally negative' towards union activities in the plant. He noted the company recognised nine shop stewards before the strike that followed GM's withdrawal and has permitted the union only four shop stewards since then. Moreover, the shop stewards are no longer free to move about the plant on union business. (Quoted from *Leaving South Africa: The impact of US Corporate Disinvestment* by Kibbe and Hauck (p. 43).

General Motors could be argued to have sacrificed the interests of their South African workers to the interests of political and commercial expediency and the main sufferers were its own employees. Apartheid was not dented at all. General Motors itself was also not much affected — its German subsidiary and Isuzu Motors in Japan, in which GM has a minority interest, will continue to supply the South African plant. In addition, there have been unconfirmed suggestions that GM has a buy-back option agreement with Delta which would enable it to repurchase the company if conditions change.

Other US companies have specifically sought to sell their South African assets to black businessmen or to ensure that the new white owners comply with a code of practice laid down in advance.

EXXON disinvested on 30th December, 1986, but instead

of selling to a local buyer, it set up a trust to own its former South African operations based on the Channel Island of Jersey, which has the advantage of not taxing trust earnings and allowing the company to appoint a protector in addition to the trustees. The trust agreement specifically does not give EXXON a buy-back option. The beneficiaries of the trust are as yet unnamed charitable organisations that serve black, coloured and Asian com-munities in South Africa. EXXON lent the trust the money to buy its South African operations, and this must first be paid back — after allowing charitable contributions to continue at the same level as when EXXON itself operated in South Africa. Once the loan is repaid, all the profits will go to the stipulated charitable objectives (these details are taken from the Kibbe and Hauck report referred to above).

The difference between the General Motors and EXXON approaches is clearly marked.

Capitalism has many virtues. It emphasises freedom and it ensures that competitive pressures produce the best products at the cheapest price. It can provide liberation to companies hedged in by government restraints and encour-agement to individuals to develop and use their talents as entrepreneurs. However the analogy with 'nature red in tooth and claw' is illuminating. We are more than animals. We are men and women who have a higher nature. We are capable of love, self sacrifice, bravery and courage. We can appreciate beauty whether this is found in art, sculpture, architecture, music or in other people. We have learned to care for those in need, not simply to trample on them. Nature, through the 'survival of the fittest' eliminates weak members of a species, allowing only the strong to survive. We, however, protect the old, the disadvantaged, the ill and those who suffer. There is much, much more to us than animals.

It should follow, therefore, that if the rule for nature is 'prosper or die', and if capitalism has the same rule, then if we acknowledge that we are more than animals and that nature's rule should not apply to human beings, so we must be willing to accept that we cannot simply allow free market pressures or the workings of a capitalist society to determine the future of individuals. Our general principle states clearly that 'People matter' — they are important as individuals. Nature and capitalism do not accept this but, in business morality as elsewhere, the argument so far has been that this is an essential principle which all reasonable human beings would accept. We have seen how this principle can be given effect within a company between directors, managers and employees. What has it to do with suppliers?

People may matter, but this cannot be a licence for a company to buy uncompetitively or to pay more for goods than if they were bought elsewhere. This is a recipe for financial disaster and, if the company fails, so would its inefficient supplier. There is, however, a case for fairness. There is an obligation on a company to treat suppliers fairly — to give them every chance to obtain business and, as far as possible, to be loyal to them. Loyalty may well involve telling any particular supplier that the goods being supplied are not of high enough quality or are not cheap enough. Loyalty may involve giving the supplier a chance to remedy mistakes; to improve production techniques, to increase quality or to lower prices. If none of these steps can be taken so that the supplier remains uncompetitive, then there is nothing more that can be done — the company must switch to sourcing its products elsewhere.

If a company is honest and above board with its suppliers and potential suppliers, then nothing more can, in moral terms, be asked. A company cannot run its suppliers' business for them, nor can they condone inefficiency or less than the best services, quality or production skills. A company's moral position is, however, thrown into question where it deceives its supplier; where it fabricates false figures to persuade a supplier that a competitor is bidding for business at a lower price than is in fact the case, where the company's managers do not keep to laid-down credit terms or where the management of the company are not honest enough to discuss with the supplier why no future orders are forthcoming.

Honesty can be an embarrassing policy. It is often not easy telling someone — particularly someone you have known or dealt with for years — that a competitor is undercutting them or that their quality is suffering. Most people, however, appreciate plain but fair speaking. They understand and can cope with honesty. Silence, lies and excuses are much more difficult to deal with. If a buyer is honest with a company which has not obtained its business, then often he or she will retain the personal relationship with the supplier. The supplier will know what the problem is and will have a chance to seek to recapture the business. Lies and deceit, even if they arise out of embarrassment, lead to personal relationships being soured and great damage being done to both the company and its supplier. This is not in the interests of either party.

The loss of business that is important to a supplier may cause initial distress or hurt, but the supplier will appreciate business realities and will know what has to be done. The situation is not hopeless — something has gone wrong and has to be put right. If, however, orders are discontinued for no apparent reason, the supplier is left perplexed, puzzled and in the dark with little idea of what needs to be put right. Openness and fairness in dealing with suppliers has much to commend it and few disadvantages. Indeed these may well be the cornerstones of a successful business relationship.

Summary
Some larger companies use their strong positions to exploit smaller companies — either by delaying payments or by exploiting their dependence. Such practices are morally objectionable. Other firms will tell lies or half-truths in order to delay payment — carefully managing their cash

flow so that suppliers are paid at the last possible moment. Accountants and managers who do this should realise that they are manipulating the lives of others and they cannot hide behind the corporate anonymity of the firms with which they are dealing. Suppliers employ real people and real people suffer if suppliers suffer. There is much to be gained from closer co-operation between supplier and customer.

Capitalism is a hard task master and, as in nature, the rule is prosper or die. Capitalism has many virtues as it will encourage efficiency and improve product quality. However just as when dealing with each other we care for the weak and the old and do not leave them to the fate that natural selection might imply, so market forces alone cannot be allowed to be the sole arbiter of company survival. At the least, suppliers must be treated openly and fairly. A company which exploits, deceives or lies to another must take some moral responsibility for the difficulties that arise.

Competition is a necessary part of the business process, but the competition should be fair (not always easy in a world where only a minority may take morality seriously). Underhand practices, such as certain forms of industrial espionage, may not just be illegal but may well be immoral as well.

Chapter Ten

THIRD WORLD INVESTMENT AND SUPPLIERS

Capitalism fosters enterprise and new developments, it ensures that the best products are produced and that inefficient companies do not survive. Surely, however, capitalism can be condemned for fostering an unequal world where the West enjoys great affluence whilst hundreds of millions are below the poverty line? It is one thing for competition to work within a country or even within the Western world, but are different issues raised once a global perspective is adopted?

A friend of mine, an enlightened and gentle Quaker teacher, told me that she had been explaining to her class about the exploitation by Western tea companies of workers in Tanzania and other countries. In many ways she is right. Western companies pay ridiculously low prices for goods produced in the Third World. Tea, coffee, cocoa, jute, flax, copper and similar primary products are produced in Third World countries and are bought at low prices by multinational companies. The wages paid to workers in these countries are only just above subsistence level. The products are shipped to the West and all the processing and manufacture (in other words all the 'added value' which comes from the various processes necessary before sale) are carried out in the West. The result is that the Third World countries and their workers are paid the minimum possible amount for their products.

If the primary products were processed and packaged in

the Third World country, with the finished product being shipped to the West, then a factory would have to be built, wages paid to production workers, office staff recruited, taxes paid on the profits made, skills developed and the Third World country would benefit greatly. As it is, these countries are kept in poverty because they have nothing to sell except for their primary products and the multinational companies ensure that prices are kept as low as possible by 'playing off' one source of supply against another.

What is worse, multinational companies sometimes buy up estates in the Third World and use these to produce 'cash crops' for export. Alternatively, local farmers may be encouraged by their own government to produce 'cash crops' which can provide much needed hard currency — this is then used to buy arms or consumer goods for the small middle-class elements in the cities. In both cases, land is taken out of the local food production chain, thus either increasing the price of locally produced food or else making less food available. In both cases, the land of poor countries is used to benefit the rich whilst the majority of local people have less than in the past.

Should multinational investment be condemned? If this investment is primarily to produce 'cash crops' or goods for Western markets and this diverts resources which the Third World country should devote to its own development, then it might appear so, but the issue is not straightforward. Inward investment into a country can produce jobs, and dramatically increase the standard of living. Almost all Third World countries actively seek such investment — the problem comes when the terms under which it is made are considered.

Certainly any multinational which goes into a Third World country and damages the ecological balance by, for instance, strip mining or deforestation is in an indefensible position. This is certainly a moral issue. For an international company to damage the environment in the interests of profit for itself and for others must be condemned — although there are always likely to be some companies in the world which would ignore such factors. It also needs to be appreciated that the host government may well encourage such practices in order to generate immediate revenue — the Brazilian programme of tree-felling in the Amazon is a case in point. At the least, however, the company concerned has a moral obligation to the community in which it operates to protect the environment as far as it is able to do so by, for instance, replanting trees on land that has been felled or landscaping ground where strip mining has occurred.

A country may borrow money to finance local projects designed to benefit a small section of the community and the country is then burdened with the resulting debt. This raises a problem which is also linked to the last paragraph. The local community is involved in any large new project which affects their area — whether or not they are consulted. They may not be overtly involved, but they nevertheless have a stake in it because it is their area, their land which is being used. Can it be morally permissible to undertake development without the approval of a local community?

Similarly can it be morally right to burden a country with debt when the people of that country have no say in its government? This question is increasingly being asked in South America where repressive and non-representative governments burdened the economies with huge mountains of debt which affect the lives of the whole population. Too often these loans were used to buy arms for the military or to finance assets outside the country for the very small and very rich top echelons of society. Is there any moral justification for Western banks insisting on repayment when the ordinary people of these countries derived no benefit from the loans and had no say in the government which incurred them and when repayment will mean economic conditions which lead to misery and degrading conditions for millions?

These are entirely legitimate and real questions. However from the perspective of the individual businessman or woman (and it is with such a perspective that this book is concerned) these are political questions for governments and the wider community to consider. Business leaders, by themselves, cannot take a unilateral stand. They represent their own companies and have a duty to these companies. They deal with customers and governments on the basis that they are legally and properly constituted. To be sure, some of these governments may be less than representative. Even in the West, the question can be asked how representative governments really are — the US presidential election with its 'image building' and Maddison Avenue packaging may not be a very good example of a free democracy at work. Margaret Thatcher's Conservative government is elected by a minority of the electorate only. The political credentials of individual regimes are, however, outside the scope of this book.

The businessman can only work on the basis that he or she is dealing with autonomous bodies and, in negotiations, seek to take seriously the interests of ordinary people in the areas in which his or her company operates. The wider political questions must certainly be discussed and business leaders need to be aware of them, but they are beyond the scope of this book and it is unlikely that individual action by companies will resolve them. To expect Lloyds Bank or Bank of America to write off its debts owing from the Third World because the governments of some of the countries to which it lent money did not fairly reflect the wishes of the people is simply not a tenable position — either practically or morally. Moral demands must be realistic and must take into account the economic systems within which companies and countries operate. Directors of individual companies simply do not have the right to ignore these systems in favour of a personal morality of their own.

The poverty of the Third World is, clearly, a moral issue and it is one about which anyone interested in ethical problems should be greatly concerned. The West has all the powerful economic reins in its hands. Finance, insurance, brokering, management, advertising and all the essential skills for business operations are kept in the West. What is more, the extent of aid given by Western countries is tiny.

The United Nations recommended ten years ago that rich countries should give 0.7 per cent of their Gross National Product in aid every year. No country, except for Scandanavia, reaches this figure. Britain and US aid has been continually cut back in real terms and in terms of its share of Gross National Product — the total amount a country produces — the latest figures are 0.22 per cent of GNP given by the US and 0.33 per cent by Britain, both figures are less than half the United Nations target and, in the case of the US, the percentage is barely a third of the recommended level.

Even the aid that is given is often in the form of subsidies to US and UK companies to help them win contracts in the Third World. In this case the aid does not really help the Third World as the countries concerned could have bought cheaper, and just as well, elsewhere. If a £35m aid grant is given so that a British rather than a German firm wins a large contract, the donor country is not helped at all as the German supplier would have produced the same goods at a lower price. There is an increasing tendency for Aid and Trade to be linked to ensure that commercial benefits flow to the donor country. This tends to result in aid going to the more credit-worthy countries rather than to the poorest of the Third World nations.

There is no question that the rich countries of the world are self-centred and greedy and that they have not taken on the burden of recognising the 'brotherhood of man' or that we are neighbours living in one world. It is true that appeals by charitable organisations raise large sums of money when disasters occur, but these are drops in the ocean compared with the need. There is also a feeling of weariness in giving in some quarters as well as an increase in the view that 'charity begins at home'.

The question is, however, whether the inequalities between First and Third Worlds have anything to do with businessmen and women, other than as private individuals who, as individuals, MUST obviously be concerned with political and financial issues that go wider than the topics dealt with in this book. It is here, perhaps, that my friend, the Quaker teacher, may be being slightly over-simplistic. Hers is, however, a common position taken by many people with a social and moral conscience and it is worth examining in a little depth.

Directors and managers have, as we have seen, various responsibilities and duties. They are primarily responsible to shareholders, who own the company, for its profitable operation and development. Unless the directors are also shareholders, they are not using their own money. They are, in effect, trustees for other people's funds. Their duty to shareholders is to maximise capital and revenue returns although, as we have seen, profit is not the only factor that they should take into account.

At the lowest level, directors and managers cannot simply give away money belonging to the company which they do not own. To do this would amount to stealing — albeit stealing to benefit a third party. To be sure, they can make charitable contributions and support good causes if this is in the best interests of the company and, unless this can be shown to be the case, they will not even get tax relief on their giving. They may well, for instance, obtain valuable publicity by doing this and hence positive commercial benefits may result.

The directors cannot, also, deliberately be inefficient. If the company has a choice between two alternatives, then if the directors knowingly choose the one that is least efficient or the one that will generate least profit, they are — unless there are special circumstances — not doing their job and may even be in breach of trust. We saw in the first chapter that directors who do not make proper use of a company's resources are likely to find their company taken over by more efficient and aggressive management.

At the end of the day, companies rely on shareholders for investment. From time to time, a company may have a 'rights issue' — existing shareholders are given the right to subscribe for additional shares in the company, usually at a price a little below the ruling market value of the shares. Investors will only put up the money that the company needs if they are satisfied that they are going to get a positive financial return. If they want to give to charity, they will do so by giving direct to charities that appeal to them.

A company cannot act as a charity and at the same time strive to increase profits and returns to shareholders. If, therefore, a company is to pay higher prices to Tanzanian or Indian tea plantations so that they, in turn, can pay higher wages to their workers, these higher prices must make economic sense. The demand for tea (or coffee, cocoa, copper or any other product) depends partly on price. If prices rise too high, demand will fall. In Turkey, as an example, there are very high import duties on instant coffee, so this coffee is regarded as a great luxury and few people buy it.

A number of nations produce coffee and tea, and they all want to sell more of their product, but they can only do so if their prices are lower or equal to the prices demanded by other countries — unless, of course, their product is of a particularly high quality which would justify a premium or if it can be promoted so that consumers are willing to pay more for it. Any country that simply puts its prices up would soon find that no-one bought its tea. Similarly any coffee importer in Europe or the US who paid more for its tea than its competitors would not be able to sell its products as they would be more expensive than the adjacent tea packet on the supermarket shelves.

Even if the producing nations get together and form a

cartel to keep prices high (and it is noteworthy that such cartels within a Western country such as the US or UK are generally illegal), then they will still have difficulty standing out against market forces. The Tin Council tried to maintain a high price for tin and ended up with enormous losses which may have to be funded by its members. Jamaica tried to corner the market in Bauxite, and came badly unstuck financially in attempting to do so.

The most successful cartel of producing nations has been the Organisation of Petroleum Exporting Countries (OPEC). The petroleum producing nations banded together and forced oil prices very high from 1974 onwards. The Western nations had no alternative but to pay far higher prices to producing nations and there was an enormous shift of wealth from the West to the oil exporters. OPEC could not, however, stand out against the market. The West economised — cars became smaller, nuclear energy reduced oil's importance for electricity generation, new oil reserves were discovered, notably in the North Sea, and demand for OPEC oil fell. OPEC introduced production quotas on its members to restrain demand, but member countries started to over-produce and the inevitable happened, prices fell so that oil prices now stand at a lower level, in real terms, than twenty years ago. There are almost always substitutes that can be produced, if prices of any commodity rise too high, and economies can be made.

Artificial manipulation of any market is generally impossible. One must say 'generally', as there are exceptions. The 'Central Selling Organisation' (CSO), controlled by De Beers, controls the price of diamonds worldwide by rationing supplies. The CSO maintains huge diamond stocks which, if released, would cause the price to fall heavily. However the CSO is so sophisticated that it trickles out diamonds through approved dealers and so ensures that a glut never occurs. So successful has this policy been that diamond prices rarely fall. The CSO's work is made easier as one country, South Africa, produces most of the diamonds in the world. Diamonds are, also, luxury items where demand does not vary directly in relation to supply. The large diamond producers, even from countries which are hostile to South Africa, like Zambia or the Soviet Union, find that it is in their interest to co-operate with the CSO.

Multinationals cannot be straightforwardly criticised for their failure to pay higher prices for primary products as, to do so, would be to act against their own commercial interests and the interests of their owners. Any director who took such a course would be failing in his or her moral duty to the shareholders concerned. Any changes that are proposed need to be brought about as part of wider political changes that must be supported, in a democracy, by the people of the country concerned.

However a more sophisticated question now arises. Should not multinationals invest more in Third World countries so that the 'added value' — processing, packaging, etc. — on these primary products is spent in the Third World? Again, we must recognise that multinationals are not charitable institutions. Might it, however, not make economic sense to invest in these countries?

Britain now has larger investments in foreign countries than any other country in the world except Japan — larger, even, than the United States. Much of this investment is, however, in Australia, Canada, Europe, New Zealand, South Africa and the United States. Britain did have huge investments in commonwealth countries such as Ghana, Kenya, Nigeria, Tanzania, Uganda and Zimbabwe. Although there are still investments in these countries, the extent of the new investment over the last twenty years has been limited. Most of the huge outflow of investment in recent years has gone to Europe and North America. Why is this? Is it because of the selfishness, greed and, possibly, racism of multinationals and the directors and managers who control them? Should they, therefore, be morally condemned?

Multinationals invest hard earned profits belonging to

their shareholders where this investment will yield good returns. Among the conditions they look for are the following:

(i) A stable political climate: No coups or left wing governments that may nationalise the investment without compensation, and a peaceful environment for business,

(ii) Either a commitment to free enterprise (if they are going to invest, they will wish to do so in a country where they will be allowed to manage their investment to best effect, without continual interference), or a strong government who will ensure stable conditions in which business can be conducted and which will remain faithful to its undertakings.

The first of these alternatives may be a democratic government whilst the second may be authoritarian — either a military government, a one-party state with a consistent record of supporting free enterprise or a communist government which maintains tight controls but is nevertheless willing to do business with Western firms in its own best interests.

(iii) A strong local economy: If an economy is strong, taxes will be low (it does not, after all, make sense to invest in a country with high taxes — this is why Britain's present low personal and company taxes are attracting inward investment) and dividends on profits will be able to be sent out of the country. Weak economies have exchange controls which make it more likely that any investment made will become 'locked in' to the country concerned and dividends on profits will not be allowed to be paid out.

(iv) A good supply of primary products; a sound infrastructure (telephones, electricity, roads, airports, etc.); a labour force that is either trained or can be trained, and access to good local or international markets for the companies' products.

Important though point (iv) is, it is not the most

143

important set of factors. Training can be given, communications can be improved and radio telephones via satellite can be installed. If, however, the first three conditions are not met, then any investment is likely to be very risky indeed — if not foolhardy. If, of course, the prospect of profits are really high, then the risks may be worthwhile, but even with the prospect of high profits, the risks of having everything taken away by a hostile government will deter all but the bravest or most philanthropic investor. We have seen that directors of multinationals cannot be philanthropists with money that belongs to someone else.

Many commonwealth countries in Africa simply do not meet the first three conditions. The governments that the people have chosen, or that have been imposed on them — many are not democracies as the West understands the word — are often hostile to the West and to private investment. This does not mean that the Western democratic system is necessarily the best. There are many different political systems and the debate between them is far outside the scope of this book. The Western parliamentary system is, it is sometimes said, essentially a European system which does not export well. It is suitable for countries that have European origins or, possibly, that share a European outlook on the world, but for few other places. Because of this, few countries in Africa are Westminster-style democracies. Most are one-party states or are countries where the government is dominated by one tribal group. These may, or may not, be the best systems for these countries, but it is not surprising that private investment (operating from within existing Western structures) stays away. One possible exception to this is Kenya which has set out to woo foreign investors and where the first three conditions above are, largely, complied with. The result is that Kenya is more industrialised; has a stronger basic economy and a higher standard of living for its people than almost any other country in sub-Saharan Africa.

South Africa, in spite of the problems of apartheid, scores

highly on all the above criteria and, therefore, has until recently continued to attract foreign investment, in spite of the headline news reports. What is more, many business-men who operate there are not convinced that doing so is necessarily immoral or wicked. Some, at least, of South Africa's black leaders continue to welcome such invest-ment, such as the Zulu leader, Chief Buthelezi. Others, of course, do not. It is sometimes not recognised that the standard of living of South African's black community is one of the highest in Africa.

This is *not* to be taken as condoning or approving apartheid. Apartheid is morally wrong — indeed it is wicked and, in religious terms, sinful. Even if the religious dimension is ignored, apartheid is still to be condemned as it infringes against our basic moral principle. In South Africa, all too often the black members of the population do *not* matter, they are *not* treated as individuals whose interests are vitally important. Saying that apartheid is to be morally rejected and condemned is not, however, necessarily the same thing as saying that businesses should not invest in South Africa. There are two issues:

(1) apartheid is morally wrong and must be morally and religiously condemned,
(2) no businessman or woman should morally support investment in South Africa.

There is often too much sloppy thinking when it comes to moral issues such as the problem of South Africa. State-ment (1) is undoubtedly true. Apartheid must be con-demned and people must be brought to realise its moral repugnance, just as people had to be brought to recognise the moral evil of slavery or of child labour — both of which were once supported by Church and moral leaders. Businessmen and women have a moral obligation to do anything in their power to prevent apartheid continuing. However (2) does not necessarily follow from (1). At the very least argument is required to show the link between these two statements. The best way to overcome apartheid need not necessarily be to stop further investment in the country.

To say, therefore, that businessmen or women who support investment in South Africa are not necessarily morally wrong, is merely to recognise that businessmen and women are realists with moral and legal responsibilities of their own. They are not running charitable institutions. This must not allow them to contravene clear moral codes — they must not allow or approve any action which will infringe our general principle that 'people matter'. However before they can be condemned, it must be demonstrated that they *are* infringing this principle. This requires there to be a link between statement (2) and statement (1) and some business people at least do not think this link has yet been made. The businessmen or women operating in South Africa and pursuing an enlightened and open employment policy, treating people from different races equally, fostering training in the black community and providing opportunities for those seeking jobs are not necessarily wicked. They can, indeed, be devoted and committed individuals with a high moral sense to whom the apartheid system is repugnant but who see the best way forward being to overcome apartheid by increasing prosperity.

New, inward investment into South Africa has fallen markedly in the immediate past as the first of the four criteria set out above are no longer seen to apply. There is no longer a stable political climate. There is increasing unrest as well as demonstrations and violence. The African National Congress (ANC) is committed to the overthrow of the present South African government and this process is likely to be long and arduous. The country will suffer and, most of all, the black population will suffer as they are on the bottom of the economic pile. South Africa's economy is growing at only 3 per cent and this is less than the rate of population increase. More and more poorly educated whites as well as the members of the black population are being thrown out of work. The result is political polarisation with some whites voting for hard-line, Nazi style tactics and the black community being less and less willing to compromise (it is extraordinary, in the face of this situation, how much goodwill and cheerfulness there still is in South Africa and how little real hatred and enmity).

These results were largely inevitable given the cut-backs in inward investment. They were readily forseeable, and a choice has to be made between two positions:

(a) continued investment into South Africa in order to increase prosperity, to cause the country to grow economically and thus to need more skilled workers. Treating the country as a member of the world community, whilst maintaining intense pressure for racial equality and for the elimination of the apartheid laws:

(b) boycotts, blacklists and a stop on investment in the hope that this will lead to the overthrow of the government and the appointment of a black or non-racial government. Previous experience in other countries in Africa indicates that one-party government or government on tribal lines would be the likely outcome when the present government falls and that the transition period would be long and bloody. South Africa has a long coastline with excellent ports and the chances of a successful embargo are not high.

The majority of the world community has opted for alternative (b), but it is, perhaps, not surprising that there are others, who are not necessarily racists bigots, or 'sinners', who take the first view. At the very least, the issue is debatable — the examples of General Motors and EXXON given in the previous chapters contain important lessons.

The Western world opposed the communist governments of the Eastern Block for forty years following the second world war. This did not, however, prevent trade nor did it prevent sporting contacts — although in both cases combined with a resolute political and military stand against the communist system. Now the Soviet Union and its satellites appear to be changing and this must be a cause for joy both inside and outside these countries. There is more than one way of bringing about change. Trade and business can help to foster moves towards a liberal and more free society.

Those who continue to invest in South Africa, or to maintain investments there, or those who traded with the communist block may believe that by so doing they can contribute to the prosperity of the countries concerned and thereby help all the population to better their living standards. To be sure, they also believe that their investment will be profitable — to invest on any other basis would be irresponsible and a breach of their obligations to their shareholders.

There is a wider moral question as to whether any country can prosper if it is dependent on charity. Certainly relief may be needed to cope with extreme natural disasters, but if a country has a basic government establishment that is hostile to private investment (Sudan is a good example), there is likely to be little 'that business leaders can do to help. Those who have chosen the socialist path are not necessarily wrong to do so — but they cannot really expect to look to business leaders in the West to help their own system overcome its shortcomings. Many Third World countries which have embraced communism have found that the system just does not work. There may be various reasons for this and one of the main ones may well have to do with the need for personal motivation and the need for individuals to see a clear link between the efforts they make and the rewards they receive. However the doctrines of centralism, state control and a stifling of initiative have frequently led to economic decline and difficulty. Almost all the countries that took this path have had to modify their positions to a greater or less degree — examples include

Russia, China, Hungry, Poland, Czechoslovakia and Mozambique.

This is *not* to say that capitalism is necessarily better than communism, still less is it to deny that a 'third way' may be possible. Nevertheless, the results of the two systems can increasingly be predicted. Capitalism *does* increase efficiency and improve quality, it also leads to the blight of unemployment and a divided society. Whether the one necessarily involves the other is an open question. Even more questionable is whether one can justify the other.

Businessmen and women in North America and Europe operate in a capitalist environment where they have to take responsibility for the decisions they make. They cannot be forced to take decisions which would cause them to breach the duty of trust they owe to the shareholders whose servants they are. The question whether the whole system within which they operate needs to be changed is a wider question which philosophers, politicians and other individuals should rightly debate. In the meantime, business life must go on!

If a country does comply with the general economic and political conditions set out above, then normally investment in this country will be attractive. Enormous inward investment has poured into many countries in Asia to take advantage of cheap labour, favourable government policies and a stable political climate. The result has been that Taiwan, South Korea, Singapore, Hong Kong and the like have boomed. In fact, so great has the boom been that some companies are already moving their plants out of these countries into others with lower labour costs such as Thailand, the Philippines and China, as the newly developed countries (NDCs) have costs that are nearly up to European standards. This, of course, is very good news for the NDCs — as it shows how well they have done — as well as for the underdeveloped countries to which factories will be moved. They will, in turn, benefit from industrialisation. Few moves are, however, made to African countries because they do not comply with the essential conditions listed above.

The standard of living of the majority of previously poor, Far East countries has improved. It is true that a minority of people in these countries do still suffer. The same applies in Western countries as well. This, however, raises a political question as to the comparative merits of capitalism, socialism and communism and this, fortunately, is outside the scope of this book. There are real questions as to whether materialism and lack of compassion necessarily always go hand in hand with capitalism. If this is so, then the price may be too high — although it first needs to be demonstrated that this is necessarily so.

The people of each country must, at the end of the day, take responsibility for their own system of government. It is a sad and terrible fact that most governments are harsh, unjust and cruel — at least to a minority of their people. It is also sad that corruption and self-interest rule amongst most politicians round the globe. These are real problems, but they cannot be solved by the businessman in isolation from the rest of society.

When, therefore, considering moral obligations to suppliers in Third World countries, it does not seem realistic to expect business leaders to resist market realities. Political changes must take place and bringing these changes about is not a task for the businessman or woman any more than for any other individual citizen of the Western world. This may seem like washing one's hands of unstable or unrepresentative governments, but it is not clear what else can be done *by the individual businessman or woman* with whom this book is concerned. Of course, at a wider political and economic level much can and must be done. It may well make sense for individuals to give generously through charitable organisations to less fortunate countries, but this will be done on an individual basis rather than through the company's bank account.

There is, possibly, a way forward. If a country whose

government fulfilled the four conditions laid down earlier in this chapter approached some of the multinationals, frankly setting out what they could offer, then there is a reasonable chance of persuading these companies to invest. Senior businessmen often *do* have a moral conscience to which appeal can be made, but they can only be expected to consider such investment if the circumstances are right and the investment is likely to be profitable. In too few countries, sadly, are the conditions right to attract private sector investment.

If the conditions are suitable, then enlightened self-interest will encourage foreign investment. It is certainly to be expected, morally, that companies should recognise a duty to participate in the development of the countries in which they operate and, indeed, it will be in their own interests to do so. What they cannot be expected to do is to act against the interests of shareholders and to turn their companies into charitable organisations.

Summary

Directors are in a position of trust — managing their companies on behalf of the shareholders who own them. They are not free to give away funds which belong to shareholders for their pet charitable projects. Investment in the Third World will depend on the right conditions for business being created in the countries concerned. When these conditions are available, then it is reasonable to expect multinationals to invest — it will be in their interests to do so.

Multinationals should invest so as to develop and not to exploit and should have a commitment to the countries in which they operate, but this commitment cannot be expected to over-ride their duty to their shareholders. However, any company which invests with profit as the sole objective and which ignores the local environment or the needs of local people deserves moral censure. Such behaviour is a form of apartheid — treating people in the Third

World as if they were a group that does not matter and this directly infringes our general moral principle.

Chapter Eleven

THE CITY

Earlier in this book, the change from a system of unwritten moral rules to tighter laws and guidelines was outlined. This was based on an increased feeling that City institutions could not any longer be relied on to follow the unwritten 'codes of the club'. However it is clear that not even the written rules are always followed — as the behaviour of Britain's biggest bank, National Westminster, makes clear. *The Economist* of January 28th, 1989, reported as follows:

> The latest scandal has tarnished the highest echelons of Britain's biggest and most respectable commercial bank, the National Westminster. . . . County NatWest, NatWest's investment-banking subsidiary, concealed the failure of a rights issue that it was handling for Blue Arrow, an employment agency. County ended up with a 9.5 per cent stake in its client, which it did not disclose for three months; as well as a $30m bill for an indemnity to Union Bank of Switzerland, which has only just come to light . . . Top NatWest managers, including Mr Tom Frost, NatWest's chief executive, knew what County was doing and were involved in the decisions to keep it quiet. . . . Last February, when NatWest was asked by the Bank of England to investigate its subsidiary, it was in fact NatWest itself that needed investigating.
>
> As the affair develops, so the damage to NatWest's reputation gets worse. . . . The big surprise of this affair is that, instead of cracking down on their subsidiary and

insisting that it come clean promptly, NatWest's top directors became involved in a cover-up. . . .

For too long, financial crime has been treated as akin to being economical with the truth on a tax return. Those days are past.

National Westminster is one of Britain's most reputable banks, and yet the directors had clearly been involved, at the very least, in questionable behaviour — concealing the failure of a rights issue by a client, presumably in order to bolster the name of the subsidiary through which this was organised, and then concealing the steps taken to conceal the failure. Moral, and possibly legal, culpability such as this will undoubtedly have to be more strictly dealt with in future and additional legislation with, possibly, much stiffer sentences for the individuals involved may well be required.

New York, London and Tokyo are the world's three great financial centres. There are, of course, other centres but these three cities span the international time zones and dominate international investment, foreign currency dealings, capital flows and equity financing. It is not, however, with these global activities that this chapter is concerned, but with the domestic obligations of a country's financial institutions.

For the sake of clarity, by 'financial institutions' I mean the banks, merchant banks, stockbrokers, dealers, pension funds, insurance firms, unit and investment trust managers and similar institutions which form 'the City'.

Twenty years ago, the moral standards of the City were exceptionally high. The London stock exchange's motto was, and still is, 'My word is my bond'. Huge deals were put through on the basis of a nod or a telephone call and the stockbroker's commitment, once given, was binding. However as we have seen, the last twenty years has seen a massive increase in the regulatory powers of bodies such as the US Securities and Exchange Commission (SEC), the London stock exchange council, the takeover panel and a plethora of bodies whose function is to regulate the activities of member firms. The role of morality has increasingly been taken over by the expansion of the legal frontiers.

Tight ethical guidelines have been laid down which almost have the effect of law. Extreme sanctions back up these guidelines — these sanctions can be financial, they can include expulsion from the umbrella of the regulatory body, which would prevent the company trading, or they can simply be the odium that comes from being frowned on by members of the club. This latter sanction is less important than it once was — what is and what is not acceptable is increasingly determined by the laid-down guidelines of the regulatory bodies. Generally, today, the sanctions fall under the first two categories as the ethical guidelines are tightly drawn and what is permitted by the rules is considered acceptable.

It is no part of the purpose of this book to rehearse the rules and ethical codes of the different bodies. Once rules or laws are laid down, then they must be complied with although, as the case of NatWest shows, this does not always happen. In the 'old' days, no commercial banking director would have sanctioned the type of behaviour that is reported to have taken place at County NatWest. In the new City environment, times have changed and there is no dispute that such practices must be stopped. Beyond the new framework of rules that will be necessary to do this, however, the moral challenges still remain and it is with these that we are concerned.

Morality is always moving beyond the rules and the regulators are always trying to catch up. The same, interestingly, can be said in the relationship between religion and morality. Religion should, ideally, always be calling us beyond the bounds of what is considered acceptable behaviour at any one time. Jesus told his followers that even thinking about going to bed with a pretty lady was a sin — not just going to bed with her.

Wilberforce led people to re-appraise morality and to see that slavery must be rejected; child-labour came to be seen to be morally unacceptable on religious grounds and, today, racism and sexism are increasingly seen to be morally indefensible positions. The frontiers of morality are not fixed, they are expanding as our knowledge and technology advances.

Twenty years ago, the ethical issues surrounding genetic engineering did not exist as science had not developed the techniques which gave rise to the problems. Sadly, many religious people do not recognise this and instead busy themselves with fighting yesterday's battles by yesterday's rules instead of recognising the dynamic nature of human existence and that the real problems are those that lie ahead.

The real moral issues affecting the City do not revolve round whether or not insider dealing should take place, whether or not one should make multiple applications for shares when a company is privatised, whether or not one should conceal failures from the investing community or break laid-down rules. The law is clear on these areas, there is no room for doubt. It is true many people still choose to ignore the law because the potential gains are great, but they know they are breaking the law and are clearly acting both immorally and illegally.

The more complicated, and significant, issues lie in those areas not at present covered by law. A few examples may illustrate this.

(1) The last five years has seen an unprecedented increase in takeover activity. One company may be taken over by another when it is not using its trading, property or other assets as effectively as it might do. The bidders consider they can make better use of the company's potential and are prepared to pay for it. There is much that is good about this system — it keeps management on their toes and ensures efficiency.

Recently, however, there has been a growing tendency for takeover bids to be made with the use of 'junk bonds'. Instead of company A offering to pay cash for shares in Company B, Company A instead offers shares or loan notes which may be more attractive than they seem.

Let us imagine that Company A has 10 million ordinary shares in issue and the market price of these shares is 800p. The company is thus valued at £80 million. Company B decides to launch a takeover bid, but calculates that it will have to pay at least £100 million if the bid is to be successful. Company B does not, however, have access to £100 million in cash. It has various alternatives if it does not have the funds available from within its own resources:

(i) It can borrow the £100 million. This means increasing its gearing — the ratio of its borrowings to its own share capital. In other words, it will have to substantially increase its borrowing — and this is not only expensive but also makes the company vulnerable. Borrowed money has to be paid back and in the event of a downturn, the bidder can get into difficulties.

If, therefore, the money is borrowed, Company B may have to try to sell off assets belonging to the newly acquired Company A as quickly as possible. By so doing it can hope to reduce the level of its borrowing. It may well, therefore, break up Company A, selling off companies that are subsidiaries. Other assets may be sold or, if they are needed for Company A's business, they may be sold to a financial institution and leased back. If Company A can be broken up and sold for, say, £130 million, then Company B will have made a healthy profit on the deal. The secret, however, of this type of operation is to break up and sell on parts of the acquired company as quickly as possible to keep down interest charges on the money that was borrowed for the bid.

The late 1980s saw a spate of Leveraged Buy Outs

(LBOs) and the consequences of the buyer borrowing huge sums of money to finance the takeover can be severe. The American company, Beatrice, sold everything from car rental to suitcases to brassieres. It was bought out in 1986 for $6.2 billion. The new management sold off $7 billion of assets including Avis Car rental, Max Factor, Samsonite and Playtex. This cut total debt owing by the company that had made the buy out from $8 billion to $3 billion. All that remained at the end of 1988 was Beatrice's domestic food operations which was proving hard to sell.

In fact, the Beatrice example is one of a buy out that has largely worked — all the companies that were sold are performing better on their own than they did when they were part of the larger group. The danger comes, however, when the buyer borrows too heavily and is then unable to sell assets to repay its debt, for instance because of a stock market fall. In the 1980s, LBOs occurred in a financial climate that ideally suited them — low interest rates and fast growth. The changed conditions of the 1990s may be a different story.

If the process of 'asset realisation' is financially driven, in other words if it is determined by the need to raise funds to clear borrowings, there is likely to be little or no thought for the jobs and lives that may depend on the assets that are realised.

(ii) The second alternative is that Company B can issue its own shares in lieu of Company A's shares. If, therefore, Company B's shares stood at 200p each, it might offer five of its own shares (5 × 200p = 1000p) for every one share in Company A. This is attractive because no money has to be borrowed. There are disadvantages, however. Company A's shareholders are not likely to find an offer of shares as attractive as cash, and so might want a higher price before they sell. What is more, all the Company A shareholders now become shareholders in Company B, and — given that they have sold out once and would do so again if a good offer comes along — Company B itself may become vulnerable to a takeover bid from a third party.

(iii) The third possibility is that Company B may offer not shares, which have the disadvantages set out above, but other forms of 'paper'. The company may, for instance, offer loan notes, repayable at some future date and carrying a good rate of interest. If the shareholders in Company A accept these loan notes, they will have no votes in Company B, since only equity shares carry votes, and they will enjoy a high rate of interest pending eventual repayment of the loan. Shareholders in Company B will enjoy all the advantages to come from the acquisition — as well as the risks.

Of course, shareholders in Company A may be nervous in that they may worry about how secure the loan notes are. These may be secured on the shares purchased in Company A or the interest rate may be so attractive that they are willing to ignore the risks. This type of procedure allows a small company to take over a much larger one, just by issuing 'paper' promises to pay in the future. Of course, if all goes well, these promises will be redeemed, but there are risks.

In particular, *all* the profits made by the newly acquired Company A may have to be paid out to finance the interest on the loan notes. This means that Company A and all its subsidiaries will be 'milked' of all the money that might otherwise have been used to develop the business and the strengths of these businesses will be diminished.

In all these, and similar scenarios, a hostile takeover bid occurs when one company takes over another against the wishes of the management of the company being taken over. Hostile bids are to be contrasted with agreed mergers or amalgamations where no moral issues may arise. In the case of hostile bids, however, management are being forced to see their company pass into other hands and, as it is the shareholders who own the company, management may have no control over the situation.

The position can therefore arise that a company may have been built up steadily over the years by dedicated, caring and competent management. The company may look after its employees, customers and suppliers, it may have a real sense of purpose within the community, it may be steadily increasing profits and dividends — and yet it can be taken over by speculators anxious to make a short-term financial killing. These speculators may have no commitment to the company or to the employees. They may have one god and that is profit, one goal and that is short-term financial advantage. People do not matter and individuals are tossed aside in the interest of greater and faster profits on 'the deal'. Sadly, this situation is becoming more and more common.

Morally, the situation is not clear cut. The shareholders own the company and if they wish to sell, they surely have a right to do so. However this is not as obvious as it may at first appear. It implies that shareholders only have an obligation to themselves to secure the largest possible financial gain and this is far from the case. Shareholders have a *much* wider responsibility — although few of them take this seriously. They have a moral responsibility to the people employed by the company and to all those whom the company affects. They are the owners, and must take the responsibilities of owners — they cannot hide behind the fact that ownership is by means of shares. *Financial criteria alone should not and cannot be the sole criteria to determine the outcome of a bid.*

So strongly do some senior managers feel about this, that calls were made at the Confederation of British Industry (CBI) Conference in 1988 for restrictions to be placed on hostile bids. Here again, we have the desire for a moral imperative to be transferred into a legal rule as the moral obligation has ceased to have any force. John Banham, the Director General of the CBI, proposed in November 1988 sweeping changes to mergers policy and the takeover code designed to slow down bids. There had been a spate of bids for British companies (Nestlé for Rowntree; Elders for Scottish and Newcastle, the brewers, and two lapsed bids — Goodman, Fielder Wattie's offer for Rank Hovis McDougall and the South African controlled Minorco's offer for Consolidated Gold Fields) and this surge had prompted the call for protection. Mr Banham said:

> Companies are not to be traded away ... by a collection of high rollers ... in some kind of economic casino.

He put forward six proposals. That:

(a) companies should have to bid for their target once their shareholding reached 15 per cent (not the present 30 per cent — see page 53);

(b) any takeover should be approved by 75 per cent of the target company's shareholders;

(c) bids which depend on high levels of borrowings ([ii] above) or from companies which are immune from a counter-bid should be automatically referred to the Monopolies and Mergers Commission;

(d) bidders should be forced to spell out plans for target companies in the form of a prospectus;

(e) voting rights should be stripped from shares bought during the bid period;

(f) offers should only be accepted with the support of two thirds of shareholders at an extraordinary general meeting and companies should be allowed to offer a 'golden share' to pension funds to protect themselves from takeover;

(g) an unsuccessful bidder should have to sell shares to

reduce their holding below the 15 per cent level and could not bid again for three years.

These proposed changes are sweeping indeed and highly problematic. In the context of some of the hostile bids that have been made they look sensible, but they suffer from real problems. A company's existing management can easily become tired and sleepy as they are sure that they are safe. They can make certain that friendly shareholders plus the company's pension fund (which they control) have at least 25 per cent of the voting shares and thereby block any possible takeover by a more enlightened and dynamic management. As 50.1 per cent or more of a company's voting shares gives control, there would have to be some provision under the above proposals that control did not become effective until the 75 per cent level was reached — thus making management still more secure from shareholder pressure and, possibly, less willing to recognise that the shareholders own the company.

More than half *Fortune* magazine's top 500 companies are incorporated in the US state of Delaware. There is a good reason for this. By having their head office in Delaware, these companies are protected from many hostile bids — on something of the lines proposed by the CBI director. Delaware has developed an approach which gives wide discretion and flexibility to company management. The UK company Grand Metropolitan found out to its cost when bidding for the US firm of Pillsbury in 1988.

Pillsbury had adopted a 'poison pill' in 1986 (without shareholder approval) whereby, if a bid took place, the minority of shareholders who did not accept the bid would have the right to buy many new shares in the company at a very low price. Grand Metropolitan obtained acceptances from 90 per cent of Pillsbury's shareholders, but knew that if they went ahead without the approval of the Pillsbury board, the remaining minority could buy many more shares in Pillsbury which would then have to be bought out — thus substantially increasing the cost of the bid. Such a procedure would be impossible in states other than Delaware or, indeed, in Europe.

Inefficient management can hide behind the protection of laws such as those in Delaware and the same would apply in the UK if the CBI proposals were to be put into effect. This would not only prevent shareholders from getting the best return on their assets but also allow inefficient management to continue in office.

Perhaps the best of the proposals put forward by the CBI is the suggestion that the level at which a bid should be launched should be reduced from 30 per cent to 15 per cent, all the others suffer from difficulties — although even this is not without shortcomings. We have here the difficulties which arises when attempts are made to resolve a moral problem with legal rules.

It is precisely because our general principle 'People matter' cannot be applied clearly here that the situation is ambiguous. The real answer lies with a high moral sense being exercised by shareholders and their being willing to recognise that they have moral obligations which go beyond their own financial self-interest. Selling out to the highest bidder is not just simply a shrewd financial move, it can have real effects on people's lives, aspirations and conduct. Shareholders need to take the wider picture into account and to recognise that their actions have consequences.

The question must arise: *What protection is there for the person or company who wishes to act morally in a world where many other people are immoral or, at least, do not share the same moral perspective?* The answer has to be 'very little'. Acting morally should, however, be its own reward. As Kant said, the moral demand is categorical, it is not based on the 'if' of 'everything turning out right in the end'.

163

Business life is not like that and, frequently, taking a high moral position may result in individuals getting hurt. There is a sad fact of business life and it makes the individual who is really prepared to stand up and be counted in the business world for what he knows to be right all the more worthy of admiration. The person who says, 'I am prepared to act morally as long as it is not costly to me or my company' is really saying that he or she is not prepared to act morally!

(2) The second major issue that needs consideration is the role that the City plays in financing companies. Any involvement with City firms is now horrendously expensive. The complexities of the current statutory and other rules, of the Stock Exchange listing agreements and the various regulations are so great that highly competent firms of accountants, lawyers and merchant bankers need to be employed. The fees of these firms are enormous. This is not to say that they are exorbitant — they have to pay high salaries to attract the right calibre of staff and their overheads are very high indeed. In relation to the amount of money being provided for large firms, then the costs of professional advisers may seem (at least as a percentage) tolerable. The position is, however, radically different for the small firm.

In many ways the City has failed to adequately come to the assistance of smaller firms who wish to raise money — although it must be recognised that it is much more effective today than ten years ago. In Britain, the Unlisted Securities Market (USM), the market for people to buy or sell shares in companies which are not yet ready for a full stock exchange listing, and the government's Business Expansion Scheme (BES) have both made access to City funds easier for smaller companies.

The BES makes it possible for individuals to get tax relief on investments in small companies provided certain conditions are met. This has been particularly attractive for higher rate taxpayers. For every £10 000 invested by a higher rate taxpayer, the cost to the indivdual is only £6000 as he or she does not have to pay the tax that would otherwise be due. The company should, therefore, receive £10 000 at an effective cost to the taxpayer of £6000. However, much of this tax saving of £4000 is, possibly inevitably, taken up with merchant bank, lawyers and accountants costs. Also, the promoters of these schemes often require attractive options over a company's shares.

In spite of this, such government sponsored schemes have opened the door to City finance for companies that would otherwise have been too small to even consider the possibility — however it is noteworthy that the initiative came from the government and not from the City itself.

It can be a real problem for a small firm seeking expansion finance in the 'in-between' stage between being relatively newly formed and being of sufficient size to justify merchant bank type advice. The only real source of money is the local clearing banks. Banks will certainly lend, subject to the necessary security, but interest rates are high and this can be a crippling cost for the young company. The small company needs capital but often cannot afford to pay out the interest cost necessarily required by borrowed money. Profits may, indeed, be there, but these profits are tied up in stock, debtors and other assets. There is a need for equity investment or for low interest loans coupled with share options to enable the 'in between' firms to find the funds they need in order to grow.

Such schemes could probably only be provided by the clearing banks — only these banks are close enough to 'in-between' companies to be able to identify the need and to offer help and advice. Once again, imagination and thought are required — stemming from a recognition that moral imperatives go beyond the recognised norms.

(3) Private shareholders rarely control companies that are quoted on the Stock Exchange — instead the control is exercised through large institutional shareholders such as pension funds; unit and investment trusts and insurance companies. These corporate shareholders control huge investments and often have significant stakes in major British and American companies. When a takeover is launched, therefore, it is crucial for the bidder to appeal to a fairly small group of institutional shareholders — if their support can be assured, then the bid will succeed, without their support the bid will fail.

A bidder may build up an initial stake of, say, 10 to 20 per cent in a target company which can act as a platform for a bid. Institutional shareholders may well hold between 20 and 60 per cent of the shares with the balance being held by private shareholders and management. Institutional support is, therefore, crucial if the bid is to succeed. Four or five institutional shareholders may hold a near controlling stake and, therefore, their support will be vital.

Often the only criterion applied by institutional shareholders when deciding whether or not to support a bid is the price being offered. The only criterion is financial. This, however, is to ignore the moral dimension entirely.

Now it may well be argued by the institutions that they have a duty to their policy holders or to investors who have entrusted them with money. They cannot, therefore, adopt other than financial criteria. In practice, however, institutions have a wide margin of discretion as to how to act — provided only that their performance is adequate. However they do have a point in saying that they are themselves under pressure to perform well in financial terms — 'league tables' are constantly compiled showing which unit trusts, investments trusts or insurance companies are the most successful.

A recent innovation has been the introduction of

'ethical trusts' which aim to invest in an ethical manner. They may, for instance, avoid investment in tobacco companies, defence contractors or companies with investments in South Africa. The investors in these trusts have a warm and virtuous glow because they are acting morally. However the situation is not as simple as this. Business morality is, as we have seen, not just a matter of avoiding investments in certain businesses — it affects relations between employees, managers and directors as well as company dealings with customers, suppliers, the community and the environment. It is not simply a matter of being passive in avoiding the wrong but of being active in pursuit of the right. Above all, it means taking human beings seriously and valuing them as persons in their own right.

Perhaps what is needed is a campaign of education to bring home to shareholders the factors on which business morality depends. 'Ethical trusts' are a good idea, but they require a wider vision — the management of these trusts must be committed to investment in companies which take business morality seriously in the conduct of all their operations. If this approach was taken then directors and managers might begin to take more seriously an ethical approach to all their business dealings.

What may be needed is a set of guidelines for an ethical approach to business. Companies could be encouraged to adopt such guidelines and to conduct their affairs in accordance with them. Any companies that do so would, indeed, then merit investment by 'ethical trusts' and be worthy of support from enlightened shareholders and institutions.

The City needs to ask itself whether its many member firms are not good examples of organisations run for one purpose only — to maximise profit. Profit is not, as we have seen, a dirty word, but the obligations of companies go wider than

167

this. There is little sense of moral obligation to the wider community or of any commitment to use the undoubted skills possessed by City firms to try to develop initiatives to help smaller companies at subsidised rates. These initiatives might well pay financial dividends in the medium to long term, but such possible dividends should not be the motive for action. A sense of obligation and of duty is important and, sadly, this is all too often lacking. Few City board rooms ever seriously consider how their skills could be employed to help the wider community in the country at large.

In some cases, as we shall see in the next chapter, companies themselves take charitable initiatives — generally, however, they respond to initiatives from elsewhere. One of the best examples of a community initiative clearly related to business is that put forward by Prince Charles. At the end of 1988, Prince Charles launched an £80 million appeal for seed-corn finance for his 'Prince's Youth Business Trust' which aims to help young entrepreneurs, turned away by the banks, to set up their own businesses.

More than £20 million was immediately pledged by British Nuclear Fuels and British American Tobacco tempted by a mixture of philanthropy and, as the Prince's fund-raising brochure says, the link with Prince Charles' prestigious name. The government has promised to double any money raised with a maximum of £40 million. The Prince's Trust will provide a comprehensive range of seed-corn finance, business advice and information, enterprise training and marketing support. More than 4300 businesses have already been supported employing more than 7800 people. Four out of five of the businesses already supported by the Trust are continuing to trade — a much higher percentage than is normal in start-up situations.

This type of initiative is imaginative and helpful, but the City itself should be actively involved in promoting projects of this type. They must be seen not as a sideline to the City's main business, not just as exercises which are 'good for the image' but as an integral part of the City's business operations. Profit is *not* the only yardstick for success and the City firms that believe it is are immoral for so doing. There are none so immoral as those who will not recognise a moral challenge. Blindness to the wickedness of slavery or to the evils of apartheid, racism, sexism or child labour is not the road to virtue. The same applies in the business sphere.

Summary
The number of laws and regulatory bodies governing the City has vastly increased in recent years so that what is permitted is coming to be regarded as what is morally acceptable. The frontiers of morality, however, lie beyond the boundaries of laid-down codes of practice. The City needs to take more seriously the moral effects of hostile takeover bids and to consider not merely financial but also human factors when deciding between bids. Shareholders must take seriously their obligations as owners of the business — they should not, ethically, decide whether or not to accept a bid solely on financial grounds.

A greater commitment to the use of the City's skills to help 'in-between' businesses is required and ways have to be found to bring the City's skills to bear in an affordable manner for smaller companies. Failure to recognise the moral challenges that business conditions today bring is, in itself, a moral failure.

A new ethical code is needed which could be used by ethical trusts and others to target their investments. This might help to raise consciousness amongst the City community of moral issues and to emphasise that 'People matter . . .'. Shareholders must begin to realise that their obligations to the companies that they control go beyond mere financial involvement.

Chapter Twelve

THE COMPANY
AND THE COMMUNITY

London has for many years been vulnerable to flooding. The River Thames flows south from its Oxfordshire source and, at times of high rainfall, the river is flowing fast. When the spring and autumn high tides occur, the water in the North Sea rises so the river water has nowhere to go. The incoming tide stops the outflow of water from the river and the Thames is in danger of bursting its banks and flooding large areas of London.

To eliminate this possibility, after many years of discussion, the 'Thames barrier' was built at a cost of £520 million. The barrier crosses the Thames to the east of London and can block the incoming tide. The ratepayers of London were asked to contribute £120 million to the cost and this was paid by the Greater London Council (GLC) out of the proceeds of rates collected from all over London. The GLC was then abolished and the completed Thames barrier was passed over to the Thames Water Authority at the £120 million figure — i.e., the figure that London's ratepayers had to find.

The government then announced its intention to privatise the regional water companies. This meant the Thames Water Authority becoming a private company. The authority's management began preparing for privatisation. Clearly this proposal would carry many benefits to the managers and directors who would be able to buy shares on favourable terms and who would become responsible for the running of a private sector company.

Thames Water revalued the barrier at £896 million. In other words, it increased the value at which the barrier stood in its accounts from the £120 million which the ratepayers of London had originally paid to the current value of £896 million. This was partly because the government insists that the water authority uses 'Current Cost accounting' — by means of which its assets are stated at their current value rather than historical cost. This results in the inflationary element being eliminated from profit.

Almost all British and US companies prepare their main accounts under the historical cost convention, sometimes with current cost accounts as an addition. Generally current cost profits are significantly lower than historic cost profits, so the government's insistence that the water authority makes a return on the current cost value of its assets ensures that water rates charged to consumers are kept at a higher level than if the historic cost yardstick was used — it also produces a higher financial return to the government.

The water authority then started charging local councils, who are funded by tax paid by London ratepayers, a percentage of the current value (£896m) of the barrier as a 'rates precept' — in other words an extra rates charge. The local councils had no choice but to pay. The argument for this was that depreciation was being provided on the barrier — this is a reasonable argument except that the barrier had already been partly paid for by the ratepayers of London. It is rather as if you bought yourself a car, and then this was taken from you and you were charged depreciation on your use of the car on the basis that eventually you would have to have a new one.

In other words, London ratepayers having paid once for at least a part of the barrier are now having to pay for it again. To be sure, this can be described as 'prudent accounting', but to the non-specialist it may seem somewhat odd.

In addition, the government has said that the barrier will

not be retained by the Thames Water Authority when it is privatised. It will, therefore, have to be transferred to the Thames River Authority. If this transfer is made at the current cost value of the barrier, then the water authority will obtain the benefit of the uplift in value from £120m to the £1000m+ figure it is then likely to be worth. This will increase the value of the water authority and, therefore, the amount shareholders will have to pay to acquire the company. The beneficiary will be the British government which will receive an increased amount on the sale. As a result, the return that the privatised authority will have to earn on its assets will be higher than would otherwise have been the case.

At a time when London's councils are desperately short of money, when many families have nowhere to live, when rubbish is not collected in some areas and when young people sleep rough on the streets of London, the political decision resulting in taking £25 million of much needed funds for something that London ratepayers have already partly paid for may be regarded as morally questionable behaviour — however sound the accounting treatment and political intention may be.

Our general principle, ('People matter') would seem to have no direct application in the above case, but the application is there. The ambiguity comes because, at first sight, it seems that the only people affected are local councils. However it is necessary to look through these bodies to the people they represent. It is necessary to appreciate how short of money many of these councils are and how much suffering could be relieved with the £25 million that is being taken away from local councils to provide for some future contingency.

Clearly, companies and corporate bodies do have a moral obligation to the community. This obligation is one of a number that directors and managers must take into account. If one travels through many countries behind the Iron Curtain or in the Third World, the extent of the pollution is alarming. Factories belch smoke, many rivers are dead and chemical waste is easily dumped. In the West we are more wealthy and can afford to be more conscious of the environment. Stringent laws are, in many cases, laid down to protect the environment against various types of pollution.

As we saw in the first chapter, however, the moral issue does not arise where laws exist. If it is against the law to dump industrial waste into rivers, then there is no moral issue — clearly such dumping is not only immoral but illegal as well. The real issues come where there are no laws but where the environment is nevertheless being damaged. The fact that something is legal, does not make it morally acceptable.

One area where this is a particular problem is within the farming community. The EEC heavily subsidises food production in the member countries of the community. The funds are taken from general taxation and certain types of food — for instance mutton and lamb, cereals, dairy products — have guaranteed prices applied to them. No matter what the demand from customers, farmers are guaranteed that they will receive a minimum price for their produce. Farmers are, therefore, encouraged to produce more and more of such food with the result that 'food mountains' build up. The EEC is now trying to reduce these mountains, for instance quotas have been applied to milk production. However the general principle still holds — the more farmers produce the better they will be paid, no matter what the demand may be for the subsidised products. Not all farming products are subsidised — poultry and pigs, for instance, are not.

Farmers are encouraged by the government to maximise yields. To achieve this objective, more and more chemicals are used to boost production of food which, in many cases, is not needed and which, when produced, will have to be stored, reprocessed or sometimes destroyed. The continuous application of large amounts of fertiliser and other agricultural chemicals harms the environment. The amount of nitrogen in the water increases, wild animals have their natural life cycle disturbed or broken and rivers become heavily polluted. Concern is being expressed about the levels of pollution which affects Britain and America's water-tables from which much of our domestic water is drawn.

In the area of North Devon where I live, there are farmers who have been warned about pollution from inadequately controlled slurry. The slurry finds its way into small streams passing through the farmers' land and kills the stream. The farmers involved give the impression of being decent, honourable citizens who probably pride themselves on their high moral standards but, when it comes to farming methods, financial factors are allowed to take precedence. Even formal warnings have little effect — the fines are small in relation to the cost of adequate control and prosecutions seldom occur.

Many farmers are faced with a choice — maximise food production to increase earnings or cut down on yields and so lower the earnings of the farm. Faced with these alternatives, it is not surprising that many farmers opt for the first alternative. The exception is the minority who cease to use fertilisers altogether and sell their products, at a higher price, through health food and similar specialist shops.

There is a moral issue here. It is the choice between on the one hand an improved personal standard of living; maintaining an already reasonably high standard of living or, in some cases, survival as a viable family farm unit all coupled with pollution damage and, on the other hand, a restricted rate of fertiliser application combined with the financial penalties that this will bring. It is partly because the principle 'People matter' does not seem to apply clearly here that few farmers are willing to recognise the challenge and fewer still do anything about it.

Our principle appears to become even less relevant when

it comes to cruelty to animals. Animals are not human beings and can, therefore, apparently be ignored. It must be recognised that our principle fares badly in this area, and yet it is an area of increasing importance. In polluting the environment, wild life is one of the first groups to be affected. The cutting down of the Brazilian rain forests is causing the extinction of tens of thousands of species of animals, birds, insects and plants. The rain forest is being destroyed to make way for agricultural land and yet this policy is fundamentally flawed. When the land is cleared, the protection of the tree-root systems are removed and the heavy rains in the region then wash the soil away. The new settlers plant crops for one or two years but after this the land is sterile and they have to move on to clear new land — leaving behind a wasted landscape.

The settlers fail to recognise that in destroying the natural habitat, they are destroying an ecology that has been built up over thousands of years and that cannot be replaced. The intricate network of interdependent species of plants and animals forms a rich, viable, long-term environment. Its destruction will lead to a semi-desert. What is more, the losers will be mankind. The resources that the rain forests could provide in terms of forest products, potential medicines from the largely unexamined fauna and flora and the rich oxygen supply created by the lush growth are permanently destroyed. The effects this will have on the human population of this planet are not yet fully appreciated, but they are likely to be very grave indeed. Many scientists have warned of the dangers, but still the de-forestation programme continues.

Are we dealing here with simply a matter of personal preference about which more than one view is possible? Man's attitude to animals has altered over the years. Whaling was regarded as a praiseworthy pursuit up until fairly recently. Whale hunters were looked at with admiration for their courage and skill. Today, however, we have come to recognise that most species of whale are amongst the most harmless mammals in the world and there is widespread affection for them. America and Russia both spent over a million dollars in trying to save two Californian whales trapped by the arctic ice whilst the media of the world followed the story. However, man's attitude to animals is selective. The British have an affection for dogs, cats, donkeys and horses — in Devon there is a 2000 acre farm dedicated solely to giving sanctuary to donkeys. In many Mediterranean countries such animals are treated with no consideration at all. They are beasts which are of value provided they have a use — thereafter they can be discarded. The Panda is cute and cuddly and millions of pounds are spent on its preservation whilst whole species of lizards, snakes, spiders and beetles are wiped out in their millions.

It is not only in the Third World and Mediterranean countries that animals are badly treated. In Europe and North America, cosmetic and other companies use animals to test their products. In the US, 20 million animals were killed for scientific research alone in 1987.

Testing for cosmetics normally results in the painful deaths of many of the animals. There are various tests performed on animals. Firstly animals may be shaved and cosmetics are applied to their skin to see what reaction is produced. Secondly some substances which are included in cosmetic manufacture are tested to see how poisonous they might be. One common test is the LD30 or LD50 test. 'LD' stands for lethal dose. A selected group of animals are fed the substance being tested until 30 per cent or 50 per cent die. Obviously the substances are unappetising, so the animals are likely to have to be fed against their will. The amount of the substance that is required to produce the stipulated percentage of deaths gives some guide to the substance's toxicity. Thirdly is a test to determine the effect that the ingredients may have on the human eye. Ingredients used in products which are likely to come into contact with the eye, such as hairspray, conditioner, sun-tan lotion and facial cosmetics, are dripped into the eye of small animals on a continuous basis to measure the damage to the eye that takes place.

Are such animal testing procedures immoral? The issue is not totally clear cut. If it was necessary to test a potentially life-saving drug on an animal to determine if it was safe, then a case could be made for this. Better, perhaps, that some animals should suffer and die and that a cure should be found for breast cancer than that no testing should take place. However where the testing is only for cosmetics, which can certainly be regarded as a luxury product, then it does seem morally repugnant that animals should have to suffer. There does seem to be an emerging concensus that experimentation on animals during such research is wrong.

One company, in particular, has recognised this and that is the British group 'The Body Shop'. Since the chain of stores started in 1976, the company has had explosive growth. It is specifically dedicated to not using *any* products which have been subject to animal testing. It regularly checks with its suppliers to make sure that none of their ingredients have been tested on animals and will, if necessary, change ingredients or change suppliers if its discovers evidence that such testing has taken place. The company publicises its stand by leaflets in its shops which give the facts about animals testing and explains the company's policy. It overcomes the need for testing by using traditional ingredients, such as honey, natural oils and glycerine, which have been in regular human use for hundreds of years. The company's own staff volunteer to test new products and it also has an independent panel of human testers available.

The Body Shop has taken a clear stand on an issue of principle. It has partly responded to public feelings but has also taken a lead. This is a good example of a company committed to changing people's perceptions. What is more, instead of this moral stand costing the company money, it has contributed to its success. It provides a talking point for the company's products, enables customers to identify with these products and provides a distinctive aura that no amount of advertising could create. It is rarely possible for a commercial organisation to change the way the whole population thinks, but it can act as a catalyst for changes that were already beginning to take place. It is not always necessary for the businessman or woman to be a follower of moral trends — it is, at least to an extent, possibly to be a leader.

The Body Shop does not stop there. It specifically encourages staff to contribute to and be involved with the 'Boys Town' project in India and encourages its customers to identify with the work that is being carried out. There are not many companies in the world who make a point of publicising the work of a Third World charity which appears to be unrelated to its main activity. The company, of course, benefits by creating a caring and friendly impression to its customers so that they feel good about buying its products but, at the same time, it is making a real contribution — not least by raising public awareness of issues that are too easily ignored. The contrast with the larger cosmetics companies is marked and, given The Body Shop's success, it is perhaps surprising that the moral lead it gives has not been more widely followed.

Careful readers will, however, have noted that I have dodged the crucial issue. Our general principle 'People matter' does not give any guidance when it comes to animal testing. Is, therefore, the principle inadequate? To an extent, it must be admitted that it is. It rests, after all, on agreement in judgement. We saw in Chapter 4 that anyone who seriously maintained that people do *not* matter can safely be condemned and rejected — they place themselves beyond the moral pale, whatever their arguments may be. In the case of animal testing the situation is not yet so clear cut. There is a developing concensus that such testing is wrong, but there is still room for disagreement about it. A case can be made on the other side. The position is still arguable. Hopefully the point will be reached where the matter is no longer regarded as an issue for debate — it will be universally accepted. The Body Shop's position is noteworthy precisely because this point has not yet been reached. They are willing to take a lead against a position that almost all their competitors accept. This is not only brave, or at least it was when the company first took its stand, but it also pays dividends in financial and moral terms.

A company does owe a duty to the community in which it operates, although it is not always easy to set out how this duty should be fulfilled or when the company has done all it can reasonably be expected to do — the commitment is, after all, potentially open-ended, the needs of the community always exceed the supply of help available. What is clear, however, is that the moral duty is a positive rather than simply a negative one. It is a duty to seek involvement, to actively promote the good of the community and not simply to be passive and to refrain from ill-doing.

There are many other ways in which a company can actively contribute to the Public Good. It can, for instance, sponsor theatrical or musical productions; it can fund expeditions to remote parts of the world; it can support a local sports team or it can provide seats for pedestrians to sit on, flowers to improve the appearance of an area or litter bins for rubbish.

Employment policy can be another major issue. One of the chief complaints of the Roman Catholic community in Northern Ireland in the 1960s was that their people found it difficult to get work. Discrimination was practised in favour of Protestant workers. Today, in England and the United States, discrimination often occurs but it may be against certain groups of people because of their origins, colour or sex. An equal employment policy whereby workers are recruited on the grounds of ability alone would seem to be an essential part of our general moral principle. To discriminate against a particular group because of colour, race, religion or sex is to devalue the group. This undermines the very humanity of members of the affected group.

A company which operates in a particular area may need to consider providing training for members of minority groups or working with schools to increase the chances of immigrant children obtaining employment. Once recruited, however, a policy of equal pay for equal work can be the only fair one. To pay one group less than another because, for instance, they are women has to be morally rejected.

Questions also need to be asked if one group is made to retire earlier than another — in Britain women usually retire at 60 whilst their male colleagues retire at 65. One of Britain's largest health insurance companies dispensed with the services of one of their doctors at a medical centre they ran because she was a woman and had reached the age of 60. All her male colleagues were allowed to continue to 65 without question. Not only is this a highly dubious practice in itself, but it was significant in this case that none of the male doctors supported their female colleague's protest about the unfairness of the decision.

Other companies contribute more generally to the community good. Allied Dunbar has, for the past 15 years, committed 1.25 per cent of its profits to community use, mainly charitable giving, with a full-time staff handling community affairs. Sir Mark Weinberg, the chairman, is co-chairman of the 'Per-Cent club'. Member companies commit themselves to giving a percentage of their pre-tax profits to charitable or voluntary bodies. Sir Hector Laing, the other chairman of the club, wanted companies to commit themselves to 1 per cent but they would not accept this and the figure has remained at 0.5 per cent.

Some companies may 'lend' one of their senior staff to a charitable organisation with the company paying the salary, to help the organisation for a period. National Westminster Bank lent one of their managers to the Bishop of London for three years; Unilever lent one of its marketing managers to London University for a year and other large organisations do likewise. The managers benefit by being confronted with a new challenge and the charity obtains help that it could not otherwise afford.

The reduction in corporation and income tax rates in Britain has led some companies and individuals to take more seriously the need to give to charity. This has traditionally been a more prominent feature of some large business concerns in the US than in Britain — possibly because Britain has had a welfare system with high taxes which has meant that the government catered for many more human needs. The lowering of taxes coupled with less emphasis on government care carries with it a need for more private and corporate action.

Allen Sheppard, the chairman of Grand Metropolitan, was quoted in *The Guardian* as saying:

> I've given more money to charity personally since (the last tax cut) than in the whole of my bloody life. There's been some very good selling by charities, and one's got more available income and so can afford to be more generous. I do think we need to be a caring society. Do-gooding is actually about economic survival. The limiting factor in the South-East is labour availability so we can't afford to have pockets of long-term unemployment. We know that in Tower Hamlets 50 per cent of the young people are unemployed; but we also know that companies like ourselves can't find people to be milkmen or work in our betting shops. Through (the government's training schemes) unemployed people are being put in touch with employers. And all these people are our customers too, so anything we can do to get society moving will come back to us in our pubs and betting shops.

Grand Metropolitan has made philanthropy an established feature of their business. The company spends between £1.5 and £2 million out of an annual turnover of £3 billion on community services — this funds a charitable trust, training schemes for the unemployed and links between business and education as well as inner city regeneration.

Laing Construction have actually appointed a 'group director, community affairs'. There is much merit in such an appointment as it can help to keep a group's moral responsibility to the community before the board. Helping the community is, however, a by-product of success. It can only be given if the company is profitable.

Charitable giving is, without doubt, important. However there is another, potentially more beneficial form of service to the community which too few companies take seriously. This takes the form of standing back, looking at pressing problems the community faces and asking whether there is any way that the company can help — not just by giving money, but by acting as an 'enabler'. If we consider the pressing needs in the UK or the US today, what would these be? The list could, of course, be a long one, but it might include some or all of the following:

1. Better housing (or, indeed, any housing) for young people or those who are unemployed,
2. Better schooling which will increase the chances of young people finding rewarding and worthwhile work,
3. Better sports facilities which will improve the health of the community; give the young an outlet for their energies and assist those who have been ill to recover.

Clearly there are many, many more possible examples, but these may do for a start. Much will depend, of course, on the industry in which a company is operating.

Let us assume that we are directors of one of Britain's largest building societies. Our society is successful. It has an excellent record. Investors money is entirely safe in our hands. Our society pays a good rate of interest and provides funds for those who wish to buy their own homes. We may ensure that care is taken at every stage of our business. We do not lend money recklessly. We ensure that the society is adequately secured for any loan it makes. We deal compassionately with those who become unemployed and cannot fund their mortgages — avoiding foreclosing on the mortgage, i.e. we avoid forcing the person who has borrowed from us to sell his house, whenever possible, and instead try to come to some mutually acceptable arrangement. We support local charities, local theatrical groups and we look after our employees. What more can we do?

The answer may be quite a lot. First we must recognise the need. We, as directors of a large building society, know all about the housing market. We know that, although the number of houses being built has increased, there are still too few units to cope with the demand. We know that many people are homeless. We know that house prices have risen very rapidly so that whereas ten years ago the average house was three times the average person's income, it is now more than five times. We know that the local councils have to house many people in terrible conditions. We are well aware of the facts. We also, however, recognise our responsibilities to those who have entrusted their money to us — we have an obligation to them.

There are, therefore, two forces at work:

1. There is a perceived need in a field; in which we are experts; *but*
2. We have our responsibilities.

The moral challenge is not to accept the second of these as an excuse for inaction. The challenge is to see whether, by imaginative and lateral thinking, there is a way to bridge the apparent gap between the two.

I am not an expert in building society management and I do not know how practical any of the schemes set out below are. However *I am* sure that there are ways in which the two positions above can be bridged. The following suggestions may not be the right ones, but if they are not then there will be others that can fulfil the need. Our building society might consider one or more of the following courses of action.

(i) If a young couple need a house, then a 100 per cent mortgage could be advanced to them, with interest only being paid on this mortgage for an initial period of, say, three to five years. The young couple would pay as much of the mortgage interest as they could reasonably afford. The balance of interest due could be made up in one or more of the following ways:

(a) If either the husband or wife has retired parents who own their own home and who will be leaving all or a part of the proceeds of their house to the couple when they die, they might be prepared to pay the balance of the interest due — if necessary from funds lent against the security of the deeds of their own house and which would not have to be repaid until both of them had died. The value of their house would be vastly greater than the interest deficit (i.e. the difference between the interest due and the interest paid), and this deficit could be comfortably left to accumulate without affecting the house in which the retired couple lived. The young couple would, legally, be required to repay the amount lent to the parents if and when they sold their new house.

(b) The local council might be persuaded to fund the interest deficit for a stated number of years — given that the alternative would be having to house the couple at public expense — possibly in return for a share in the profit on the house when it is sold.

(c) The building society itself might be willing to 'roll-up' the interest deficit in return for a share in the profit on the house when it is sold. Failing this, private investor's might be willing to pay the interest on a similar basis — trusting that the amount of the interest that they pay would be comfortably exceeded by the increase in the value of the house.

(ii) Instead of the young couple having to buy all the house, an arrangement could be made under which half the house is purchased and half is rented. The rent would be at a recognised level and this would be paid to the building society as owner of half of the house (this is already being done in some cases).

(iii) The building society might provide specific help in a run-down area to assist a young couple to buy a derelict flat or building and then to help them to renovate it themselves. At present, a house has to be in a 'mortgageable condition' before building societies will lend — the result is that builders and speculators buy up derelict houses, renovate them and take a handsome profit when they are sold on to the first-time buyer. Funds could be made available for the materials the young couple would need, and they would provide as much of the labour as possible — bringing in skilled workmen only where necessary. Supervision by the building society would be required, but the young couple would be enabled to own a home of their own by their own efforts. No, or very low, interest would be payable until the house was completed— the balance simply being added to the amount of the loan. The society would still be comfortably secured as the value of the house, after taking account of the 'free' labour put in, would be considerably greater than the purchase price plus the cost of materials.

(iv) Co-operation could be arranged with a local council to enable 'self-help' groups to build their own houses on land provided by the council at very low cost. The council would take a percentage of the profit on the house when it was sold — in return for the land provided. The same arrangement could also apply to land owned by large companies — planning permission being granted on condition that such an arrangement was entered into. The company would get the benefit of the value of the land in due course, but in the meantime housing would be being provided.

(v) The building society might provide funds to enable several couples to come together and convert a house into several flats — the work being done largely by the individuals involved but with specialist help where required. Again, those involved would get the benefit of low prices and of putting their own labour into the flats, rather than being unable to buy the finished units from a builder as the price was out of reach.

Of course, not all these schemes would work. There might be losses. However building society managers and directors have much experience and the moral obligation and skill comes in trying to seek solutions to difficult problems.

The same approach could be developed by any company — depending on its particular expertise. Accountants, for instance, could easily fund and staff, on a voluntary basis, a financial advice centre which would work with the Citizens Advice Bureau and other voluntary agencies to give advice to individuals who had got into financial difficulties. Many poorer people do not know how to manage their money and become embroiled in a web of debt from which there may seem to be no escape. An accountant could quickly analyse the problem and make suggestions as to possible solutions. Such a service would be inexpensive to operate and would fill a real need — but to the best of my knowledge it is nowhere available.

The crucial issue is whether the will is there — the will to be active in search of solutions rather than passive in acceptance of supposed impossibilities.

A failure of will is a moral failure. Failure to act is just as much a moral failure as to act wrongly. Inaction is certainly not a recipe for virtue. Virtue, goodness and care for others are active notions and seldom are these given a high priority on individual or corporate agenda.

Summary

Companies and other corporate bodies as well as employees, directors and managers do have an identifiable moral obligation to the communities and environment in which they operate. This moral obligation goes beyond what the law demands and extends to using the resources of the company, not simply with a view to profit but also to meeting community, environmental and other needs in imaginative ways to which the resources and skills of the company are best adapted.

Morality is not just about refraining from certain actions. It demands a willingness to be active and for directors, managers and employees to take seriously the needs of the community.

Certainly directors have duties to shareholders but these should not be used as an excuse for inaction. Companies should rather be willing, by using imaginative and lateral thinking, to bridge the gap between responsibilities and perceived needs. Charitable giving by companies is right and proper, but moral obligations do not stop at writing cheques — however sizeable.

Chapter Thirteen

RELIGION, MORALITY AND BUSINESS

Once upon a time there was a rich man who had land which bore good crops. He began to think to himself, 'I haven't anywhere to keep all my crops, What can I do? This is what I will do', he told himself. 'I will tear down my barns and build bigger ones, where I will store my corn and all my other goods. Then I will say to myself, Lucky man! You have all the good things you need for many years. Take life easy, eat, drink and enjoy yourself!' But God said to him 'You fool! This very night you will have to give up your life, then who will get all those things you have kept for yourself' [Luke 12: 16–20].

So far in this book, religion has not entered in at all. When we sought a general principle of morality which could be applied in the business arena, we found it within Kant's philosophy. This principle does not depend on whether or not God exists, although it is very close indeed to Jesus' command to 'Treat your neighbour as yourself'. The injunction that 'People matter . . .' does not require a belief in God or membership of any particular religious grouping to make it valid. This is important, as otherwise the morality of the religious person and the non-religious person would be essentially different.

Kant himself considered that practical reason led one to postulate the existence of God. He thought that everyone sought the *Summum Bonnum* (or Greatest Good) in which virtue coincided with happiness. It is clear, however, that in this life virtuous people are often ill-rewarded for their high moral standards, so Kant suggested that we must postulate a life after death where the scales of moral justice were made even — the just being happy and the unjust otherwise. Modern philosophers have, as we have seen previously, asked whether the idea of an after life does not undermine morality as it holds out a 'carrot' or incentive for an individual to be virtuous. Goodness, they have maintained, should be its own reward. The argument, therefore, that God is necessary if morality is to make sense can itself be challenged.

The religious person may believe in God (this is not necessarily the case — a Buddhist is certainly a religious person, but does not believe in God, at least in a straightforward sense). However this belief should not affect moral behaviour. Some believers may, of course, not accept this. They may say that morality depends on God. The question as to whether or not morality comes from God is expressed in the 'Euthyphro dilemma' which was first put forward by Plato. The issue is simple:

> Does God love what is good, or is whatever God loves good simply because He loves it?

If God loves what is good, then the standard of what is good or bad is independent of God. This is important, as most believers claim that we should follow God rather than the devil not because God is more powerful (this would be a very weak reason — it would justify, say, following Hitler in the days of Nazi Germany because he was the most powerful figure) but because God is good whilst the Devil is evil. If this is, indeed, the case, then goodness must be independent of God and we can judge God's actions as being good by reference to this independent standard.

The alternative view is to hold that whatever God loves becomes good simply because God loves it — on this basis the slaughter of innocent people in the Old Testament (ascribed by the Old Testament to God in passages such as Joshua 11: 20) is good simply because this is what God wants.

The debate between these two alternative positions has been with us for 2500 years and is still very much alive. Fortunately, however, it is not central to our general principle since, whatever its source, we have seen that people can accept the general principle of morality established in Chapter 3. This general moral principle rests on agreement in judgement and we do not need to share a common view as to its source. Even atheists accept that beating up old ladies for pleasure or abusing young children is wrong.

The believer may claim that, in the absence of a life after death, morality does not make sense. This, however, if accepted, would undermine the moral demand. If the believer only acts morally from hope of a reward after death or from fear of punishment, then he or she is not being moral. Christianity has always maintained that one should do God's will out of love for God and not from fear of punishment. The religious person may, of course, claim that God's will is that we should act morally, but the motive for good actions should be love rather than potential rewards or punishments. The hymn writer puts it this way.

> O Lord I love thee not because
> I hope for Heaven thereby
> Nor yet from fear that loving not
> I may forever die.

If morality is hypothetical, if we only act well because of some ulterior motive then, as we saw in Chapter 4, this is not true morality. Good actions must be done for themselves alone.

The existence of God should not necessarily have a direct effect on the way that an individual behaves. Having said this, it may be accepted that, in practice, religious believers who are conscious of the presence and love of God in their lives, may well take moral demands more seriously than others. However there is no need for this to be so. There are many loving, caring, just and compassionate humanists and atheists. Christians have no monopoly on virtue.

Major figures such as Socrates, Aristotle and Gandhi have sought to show people the merit and rewards of a virtuous life — but these rewards came from the value, in itself, of this sort of life. These moral leaders did not claim that people should be virtuous to secure a reward but that virtue was its own reward. The life of egotism, of selfishness or of greed will inevitably eventually lead to misery, loneliness and unhappiness. In Jesus' parable of the rich farmer who pulled down his barns to build bigger ones and looked forward to a secure future of leisure and ease, Jesus might well have said that this sort of life would be empty and would provide no satisfaction at all.

If one looks at the lives of many retired people, they have little purpose. They have built up their own material prosperity but, when they come to retire, they find the years stretching ahead as they wait for death and these have to be filled with golf, travel, bridge, television or the garden. There is little real centre to their existence. Many business people concentrate solely on business success and climbing the corporate ladder. They measure achievement not in moral terms but in terms of the prosperity they have achieved, the type of car they drive, the house they live in, the type of schools to which they send their children and the reputation that they have within the business world. These, however, are not what is really important in life. The religious person claims there is something more.

We have, therefore, the following position:

(1) Business morality, as argued for in this book, does not depend on a particular religious position. The principle that 'People matter . . .' should be common to everyone and does not rest on presuppositions about the existence or otherwise of God or a life after death,

(2) The religious person (specifically, in the West, the Christian) will claim that, although someone who does not believe in God acts morally and correctly, something is nevertheless missing. The missing component is the awareness of God's presence and the recognition that life is about developing a love-relationship with God which will continue after death and which shows forth in love and care for others. This missing ingredient is essential for human wholeness and may transform an individual's outlook on central political and economic issues such as the relative wealth of the West and the poverty of the Third World.

(The consequences of this view are set out in my book (*And If It's True?*, Marshall Pickering, 1988))

In Jesus' teaching, the second commandment *is* second. The first is to 'Love the Lord your God with all your heart, and mind and soul'. After this comes the commandment to love one's neighbour. It follows, therefore, that the essential difference between the religious and non-religious businessman or woman will not be in their ethical approach (since they both share acceptance of the second commandment — as set out in our general principle derived from Kant's Categorical imperative). The religious person, will centre his or her life on God. Business will not be the central focus in life. Indeed too great a preoccupation with business may mean that the first commandment is relegated to second place. Here lies a dilemma.

For the Christian, the first commandment is first and this must be taken seriously. Christianity does not amount to running a business flat out all week and then going to church for an hour on Sunday, nor does it amount to simply trying to be fair in business dealings. It is much more challenging and difficult to live up to than that. A religious perspective on life may demand a total change in an individual's world-view and this may well lead him or her to reject the political systems which society generally accepts. In South America, for instance, liberation theologians take this position — rejecting the political status quo which oppresses the poor, and instead working for social and political change. In Britain, some churches are becoming increasingly involved with work in the inner cities (for instance the Church of England's 'Urban Fund' or the Jesuit Volunteer Community — the Salvation Army has always been primarily orientated in this direction) whilst other individuals feel called by their God to take the 'option for the poor' — identifying and living with the poorest members of society. Religious demands may, therefore, go considerably beyond the field of business morality, and this book is limited as it is solely concerned with the issue of business morality — it fails to address the wider political questions which may well throw into question the basic assumptions that many business people make. At the least, if a person chooses a job or career that means he or she must be wholly preoccupied with business success to the exclusion of an awareness of God, then this makes a mockery of Christian commitment.

The Second Vatican Council said that followers of Christ must avoid a tragic separation between faith and everyday life. They can neither shirk their earthly duties nor:

> . . . immerse ourselves in earthly activities as if these latter were utterly foreign to religion and religion were nothing more than the fulfillment of acts of worship; and the observance of a few moral obligations. (*Second Vatican Council: Pastoral Constitution on the Church in the Modern World 43*)

Economic life is the place where religious faith should be lived out. It is in the believer's business life that neighbours are to be loved, temptations confronted and the thirsty and hungry cared for. The believer maintains that this cannot be done adequately unless the individual is aware of God and of the love of God for all humankind.

Jesus told the rich young man who had kept all the

193

commandments from his youth that he should sell all he had, give the proceeds to the poor and follow Him. Jesus had put his finger on the young man's problem — he was more attached to his money than he was to God. He was morally good, but he had centred his life on money. This is the case with many business people who claim to be Christians today. They manage to convince themselves that it really is God's will that they should carry on building up a bigger and bigger business and, in so doing, they relegate God to second place. It is perfectly understandable that they should do this, since the alternative may be too challenging and uncomfortable. The rich young man and the affluent farmer could not face up to the religious demand — they chose to ignore it, and had to take the consequences.

There is, however, a potential problem as to how the teachings of Jesus are to be given practical effect in the business world. It is not easy to make the transition from the parables to business dilemmas. This difficulty is not helped by lay people having to live and work in the business arena with all the pressures and problems this entails, whilst priests and theologians, who claim to speak on behalf of God, live in a secure and problem free environment removed from business realities. Too seldom do the latter have any real knowledge of the pressures and dilemmas the manager, employee or director has to face.

I work in a splendid and unique college where most of my colleagues are caring, committed and dedicated priests or people in religious orders. Few of them have ever been involved in business, let alone have had to accept responsibility for the lives of hundreds of people in a group of companies. They come from a secure and comfortable existence where the future is undoubted and they have no financial worries or material troubles of any sort; from a background of seminary training, academic certainties and solutions where black and white can sometimes be kept distinct. Their theological skills and personal depth are profound — but these virtues may be of little help in deciding between business complexities.

This gulf between priests and theologians on the one hand and the real world on the other was, for me, illustrated by possibly the most important single report on economic activity to be produced by a Church in the Western world. The Roman Catholic bishops in the United States produced a long and detailed report in 1987 entitled *Economic Justice for all*. They researched the report with great care, moving across the US and their staff talked to a very wide variety of interest groups both within and outside the churches. The consultation process was nothing short of tremendous. The result is a weighty, carefully considered report full of theological depth. There are, however, questions that need to be asked.

The general message of the report in no way goes against the central precepts of this book. It places great emphasis on the dignity of each individual and the importance of all human beings. It sets out six fundamental principles:

(1) Every economic decision and institution must be judged in light of whether it protects or undermines the dignity of the human person.
(2) Human dignity can be realised and protected only in community.
(3) All people have a right to participate in the economic life of society.
(4) All members of society have a special obligation to the poor and vulnerable.
(5) Human conditions are the minimum conditions for life in community.
(6) Society as a whole, acting through public and private institutions, has the moral responsibility to enhance human dignity and protect human rights.

These are worthy aims and they are fully in accord with the general principle established in Chapter 3 that 'People matter'. However, by stressing society and community, there is a real danger that individuals may feel no personal need to act. As individuals, they can always imagine that the matters under discussion are someone else's concern. They can share the general aspirations and do nothing to bring them into effect. 'Society' [(6) above] cannot have moral responsibilities — only individuals can have these and they must exercise these duties within the society in which they live.

To understand the bishops' report, it is first necessary to appreciate the emphasis that the Roman Catholic Church today seems to place on the idea of community. Indeed to be a Catholic seems increasingly to be seen as to belong to the Catholic community and to participate in Catholic sacraments and rituals — this was not always the case in the past as the mystical writers such as St John of the Cross, St Ignatius of Loyola, St Teresa of Lisieux and others testify.

The non-Catholic model of Christianity (and, I suggest, the more traditional Catholic model) tends to see the individual as central and the individual in relationship with God as being primary. Out of this relationship should flow love for and care of others on an individual basis. There are real dangers on this approach as religion can become too much an individual affair with participants not being sufficiently concerned with the people with whom they live. The Catholic Church, today, seems to increasingly reject this model and instead puts the community first. The identity of individuals is seen as being founded in community. The world is seen as the free gift of God and what God wants back is not ritual but mutual love. The Church therefore calls its members not just to give money but to help those who are structurally poor to participate more fully in the wider community. The call is to help the marginalised of society to take a full part in the life of the community and, by so doing, to share the fruits of the community's success. The Church community is called into solidarity with those beyond its boundaries. God is found at the centre of the community and it is by building up the community that we do God's will. God is to be found not so much in a remote heaven but within the community.

This is an appealing and important vision. It rejects too great a stress on individualism and the compartmental-isation of our lives. Instead it sees God as present with us in our earthly strivings and it does not reject these strivings as being in any way of secondary importance. However the aspirations that the American bishops' report loftily sets forth are ambiguous. Paragraph 115 can serve as an example — it includes the following:

> Support of private ownership does not mean that anyone has the right to unlimited accumulation of wealth. Private property does not constitute for anyone an absolute or unconditioned right. No one is justified in keeping for his exclusive use what he does not need, when others lack necessities.

This is fine as a general principle, but what does it mean? The Catholic millionaire can happily read this, assent to the general principle but feel that *he* is not affected. After all, he may consider, his needs are considerable and he pays his taxes.

By stressing the importance of community, there is a danger that individual responsibility is thereby diminished. 'The Nation', 'The Government', 'Society' or 'The Com-munity' may be exhorted to act and we may all agree with this, but this does not touch us as we go about our routine tasks — dealing with employees, customers and suppliers or seeking to cope with the pressures and problems that every day brings to the businessman or woman.

The objectives of the report remain at the level of lofty aspirations, with little or no consideration as to how they are to be brought into being. As an example, paragraph 165 includes the following:

> Across the nation, in every state and locality, there is

197

ample evidence of social needs that are unmet. Many of our parks and recreation facilities are in need of maintenance and repair. Many of the nation's bridges and highways are in disrepair. We have a desperate need for more low-income housing. Our educational systems, day-care services, senior-citizen services and other community programmes need to be expanded. There are many other areas of our national life that are areas of unmet need. At the same time, there are more than eight million Americans looking for productive and useful work. Surely we have the capacity to match these needs by giving Americans who are anxious to work a chance for productive employment in jobs that are waiting to be done.

No one could take exception to these aims, but how are they to be implemented? In the 1988 presidential elections the two candidates totally failed to give any adequate account of how the far more fundamental problem of the US deficit of $140 billion is to be tackled, let alone to set out how the worthy objectives detailed above are to be realised. Indeed they closed down possible options that might have solved the problem such as raising taxes.

Theologians and politicians may put forward admirable objectives but it is the economists, accountants, entrepreneurs and business people who will bring about the transformed society. It could be argued that it is the businesswoman or man struggling to start a new business or to keep going an existing company or group in the face of severe competitive pressures; the individual director or manager dealing with employees, suppliers, customers and the local community that will transform society. To be sure these individuals need to be challenged and they need to be brought to think — but they must decide what they, individually, are going to do. The theologian's exhortations are so broad and the range of possibilities so wide that the challenge to the individual can be blunted.

Of course the community is vital and of course the individual can only be understood as part of the community. However it is the individual who acts, the individual who is challenged and the individual who must decide on priorities — with the realisation that he or she must accept the consequences of so doing. It is the individual who is called into a relationship with God and the individual who must show this love to those individuals with whom he or she comes into contact. The first commandment in Christianity still remains first. We, as individuals, are called to love God — it is not the community who must do the loving but individuals!

The real value of the Catholic bishops' exercise lay, perhaps, not in the report but in the consultation process which may have brought individuals to think for themselves about the issues and then, possibly, to act. If this formed any part of the intentions of the bishops, then this book shares a similar aim. Certainly anyone who claims to be either moral or religious must be willing to take seriously the needs of the poor, the homeless, the lonely and the hungry. To fail to do so whilst we remain in great comfort is a denial of our common humanity. It was easy for the Germans in the Second World War to ignore what was happening to the Jews in their midst and they were morally condemned for doing so. Similarly the person who ignores the needs of the marginalised members of our society or of the wider world or who, during a dinner party, expresses her concern but fails to act may be in no better position.

Christianity is not hostile to personal possessions or to capitalism. However it is and must be hostile to the idea that business or money should be placed at the centre of our lives. This, it claims, is the fundamental mistake made by many people. They seek meaning and purpose in their lives solely in the material world and, at best, 'fit God in' on Sundays. This is not Christianity. It may, indeed, be argued that true freedom requires us to have some personal possessions as only if we have the basic essentials of life within our own control will we be truly free. Emil Brunner, the Swiss theologian, is quoted in Brian Griffiths' book *Morality and the Market Place* (Ecclesia Books) as follows:

> The man who has nothing at his disposal cannot act freely. He is dependent on the permission of others for every step he takes. . . . Without property there is no free personal life. Without property there is no power to act, . . . And the word 'property' must be taken literally as ownership or, as we say today, private property. Without private property there is no freedom.

Care is nevertheless required here as it is easy to move from saying that there is nothing wrong with personal possessions to saying that making money and financial success the aim in life is acceptable. This move Christianity must and does reject — although it is often not made sufficiently clear that the move is illegitimate.

This book is concerned with business morality and this morality can be understood and discussed without recourse to religious categories. To be sure, we should all ask ourselves whether we live up to the high moral standard that our general principle requires and we must constantly challenge and question ourselves by asking whether there is not more than we could do. *If*, however, we also claim to be Christians or to believe in God, we need to ask ourselves a second question — whether or not we place God at the centre of our lives and whether this transforms our outlook on the world. This is even more difficult and uncomfortable as it may involve questioning and possibly even rejecting the political and moral assumptions which our society accepts and instead working for a transformation. However, unless we are willing to face this challenge then it is a mockery to call ourselves Christians. We may fail to live up to the vision of love and moral concern that Jesus set us, but if we fail to even recognise that the demand exists, then we have not begun to understand what Christianity is about.

Christianity may well require us to turn away from too

great a preoccupation with business and to found our lives on the love of God rather than material prosperity. For many people the price may be too high and they will seek to have *both* a successful business life *and* Christianity — making God like the cherry on the top of the cake of a happy and prosperous existence. Continually, however, Jesus warned that *both/and* was not an option. It was a question of *either-or*. Each of us, if we claim to be Christians, has to make a choice, and the choice may well be a painful one. It may be a choice of putting God first or our business. All our friends and colleagues may say that we are mad or fanatical if we choose the former — but a love affair without passion is a contradiction in terms and love has never been the most rational of relationships. The Christian needs to ask him or herself where the centre of life lies. If the answer is at the office, then this is a sure test that, religiously, life has been misdirected.

If you, the reader of this book, feel that you do not live up to the moral demands that you see to be present in your business life, then you can be confident that you are in the company of most people in business as well — although if you have at least recognised the failure this is a major step in the right direction. Our failure may well be part of our humanity. However it is one thing for us to fail to care sufficiently for others, to fail to take seriously that 'People matter . . .' and that every individual is important. It is quite another matter if we do not even try. If we do not make the attempt, if we do not make a real effort in the day-to-day conduct of our business affairs to be just, fair and equitable in all our dealings, to treat those we deal with as persons of great intrinsic worth, then we diminish ourselves as human beings.

We are not industrial robots, we are not slaves to our business. We are free individuals who glory in the name of human beings. We can make moral decisions and, as we go to work tomorrow, we will have ample opportunity to give effect to whatever good resolutions we may make. Whether

201

we believe in God or not is a matter for each of us to decide. However we should all be willing to recognise the moral demands that our business life makes on us and to make the attempt to do something about them.

The choices are ours.

Questions for Consideration

Chapter One

(1) Does immorality depend on knowing or suspecting that one is involved in an immoral action?

(2) Is it immoral for one company to launch a bid for another and then 'asset-strip' the company? If so, why? If not, why not?

Chapter Two

(1) Should someone in business simply obey the law, or are there moral obligations which go beyond what the law requires?

(2) Is it better to have simple company accounts which anyone can understand, but which can be easily manipulated to show what management wants, or to have complex rules governing the preparation of accounts which mean that few can understand the final result?

(3) Is it morally right that British Airways' Concorde fleet should be included in their accounts at a nil value?

Chapter Three

(1) (a) All politicians are dishonest
Margaret is a politician
Margaret is dishonest
   (b) Stockbrokers are only interested in money
Jack is only interested in money
Jack is a stockbroker
Are these conclusions true or false? If one or other of both of them are false, is this because one of the premises are false or because of a flaw in the logic of the argument?

(2) If you were asked to *prove* to a sceptic that what you use to turn the pages of this book is a hand, how would you do it?

(3) Could it ever be morally right to beat up old ladies for pleasure on Sunday afternoons; to sexually molest young children or to defraud old people of their life savings?

Questions for Consideration

Chapter Four

(1) Can the ends which we seek always justify the means we may need to use to achieve these ends?

(2) If there has to be a balance between the pleasures of one group and the needs of another, how might 'needs' be defined?

(3) If someone acts in a certain way in order to achieve some wider result (for instance being kind to people in order to impress the neighbours or being honest in order to get to heaven), is this morally good behaviour?

(4) Is the general principle: 'People matter, they are important. Treat others as you expect to be treated' a moral principle that all should accept?

Chapter Five

(1) Does a high moral stance by a company usually result in increased profits? If so, why? If not, why not?

(2) Why might the work of an arbitrageur be regarded as (a) morally praiseworthy and (b) morally culpable?

(3) Which of the following statements are closer to the truth?
   (a) The one and only social responsibility of business is to increase its profits.
   (b) Profit is our reward for serving society well. Indeed profit is the means and the measure of our service — but not an end in itself.

Chapter Six

(1) Are there ever any circumstances which would morally justify an employee in breaking the law at his or her employer's request?

(2) Is it morally justifiable for a car mechanic to 'patch up' a car that is going to be sold at auction, even though he knows that a major engine fault is being concealed?

(3) In what circumstances could it be justifiable for an employee to make private telephone calls from her office or to copy the minutes of a charitable organisation of which she is secretary on the firm's photocopier?

(4) Select any manufacturing company you know. In what ways are the production workers treated as human beings and in what ways are they treated as robots? What might the benefits be to (a) the company and (b) the employees if changes were made? What might these changes include?

Chapter Seven

(1) What does it mean for a company to be successful?

(2) Are there moral advantages in the executive directors of a company being responsible to a board of non-executive directors?

(3) What are the moral obligations of directors of a company to the company's employees?

(4) Are there any circumstances in which morality becomes a luxury that the businessman or woman cannot afford? If there could be such circumstances, what might they be?

Chapter Eight

(1) Is it morally acceptable to sell sub-standard tyres to Third World countries at low prices?

(2) Have the directors of Barclays Bank or Bank of America any moral questions to answer regarding their promotion of VISA cards? What are these questions and what might the responses be?

(3) Is there any inherent moral problem in being a director of:
(a) British and American tobacco?
(b) McDonnell Douglas (a leading arms manufacturer)?

(4) Provided potential customers are warned of the risks, should a supplier be morally free to provide any product or service? Are there any products or services which should not be supplied (e.g., cigarettes, cocaine, alcohol, missiles, credit, etc.) or which should be subject to special conditions other than those imposed by the law?

Chapter Nine

(1) Is it morally justifiable for a company to take the longest possible period of credit from a supplier irrespective of the credit terms?

(2) In what senses might industrial espionage be regarded as morally acceptable?

(3) Are capitalism and natural selection similar in being guided by 'the survival of the fittest'? Is this an appropriate moral principle and, if not, how does it need to be modified?

(4) Can it ever be morally permissible to pay workers at pay rates which are below the poverty line?

Chapter Ten

(1) Are Western industrial companies morally to blame for their failure to invest in the Third World?

Questions for Consideration

(2) Morally speaking, should the directors of tea companies pay a higher price for tea leaves to the farmers who grow the tea in the Third World?

(3) Can investment in South Africa be morally justified? If so, how and if not, why not?

(4) Is it (a) morally justifiable and/or (b) likely to be effective for Third World producers of primary products (such as copper, iron ore, tin, cocoa, coffee, etc) to enter into a co-operation agreement to force Western companies to pay a higher price for their goods?

(5) Can the businessman or woman help countries whose government is hostile to private investment or where such investment carries risks that are disproportionate to the potential rewards? If so, how?

(6) Consider some reasons why investment in Tanzania, Mozambique, the Sudan, Uganda, Ghana and Vietnam is low even though they have ample and cheap labour.

Chapter Eleven

(1) Should rules be introduced to make it more difficult for hostile takeover bids to take place? What would be the disadvantages of such a step?

(2) Should a full bid have to be launched for any company in which a potential bidder has acquired 15 per cent of the voting shares?

(3) If (a) a City institution or (b) a private shareholder has to decide whether or not to support a hostile takeover bid, should factors other than the price being offered be considered? If so, what factors? If other factors should be taken into account, could it ever be right for a City institution to turn down a higher bid on other than financial grounds?

(4) If you had to draw up a set of guidelines for an ethical approach to business to be used by an 'Ethical Investment Trust' in deciding in which companies to invest, what would be the main items to be included?

(5) Should individuals expect legal protection from the consequences if they act in accordance with their conscience?

Chapter Twelve

(1) Is it ever justifiable to make animals suffer in the interests of research? If so, what are the criteria that would justify this?

(2) What are the most effective ways of a company helping the community?

(3) Identify any *one* community need and then suggest how a company might help to meet this need other than simply by making a gift of money.

(4) If a company obeys the law, behaves properly to employees, suppliers and customers and does not pollute the environment, has it fulfilled its moral obligations?

(5) What are the advantages and disadvantages of a company appointing a director with specific responsibility for community affairs?

Chapter Thirteen

(1) Should the morality of a religious believer be different from that of a non-believer?

(2) Would the existence of an after-life undermine the moral demand?

(3) What content can be given to talk of the community having moral responsibilities?

(4) Has religion anything to do with business? If so, in what respects?

Index

Accountants 9ff, 186
Advertising 97ff
Animal rights 175ff
Arbitrageur 51
Arms manufacture 112
Armstrong, William 92
ASC 11
Asset strippers 5/6
A.T. & T 81
Auditors 4/5, 9ff
Ayer, A. J. 39
Banham, John 161
Bank of America 137
Bank of Credit and Commerce 1
Bank Secrecy Act 2
Beatrice 158
Bible, The 29ff, 46, 188ff
Body Shop, The 177/78
B.P. 52
Brazil 136
British Aerospace 7, 89
British Airways 14/16
British Coal 14
British Rail 7
Cadbury Schweppes 81
Capitalism 130ff, 148/151
Cash flow 115ff
Categorical imperatives 42ff, 192
Central Selling Organisation 141
Chairmen 82/3, 87, 109
Church Urban Fund 193
Community 170ff, 196ff
Control Data 55

Conscience 62ff
Construction Industry 70
Credit cards 101ff
Cummins 56
Darwin 123
Dayton Hudson 55
Debenhams 17
Delaware 162/3
Deming, Edward 72
Descartes, Rene 23
Dewey, John 39
Directors 76ff
Dunlop 17
Drug Trafficking 1/2, 100
Emotivism 39
Empiricism 22
Employees 58ff
Ethical trusts 167
Euthyphro dilemma 189
EXXON 129/130, 147
Farming 63, 173/4
Ford Motor Company 81
Freedom 69, 71
Friedman, Milton 55
General Motors 81, 129/130, 147
God 96, 189ff
Grand Metropolitan 181
House of Fraser 17
IBM 120/2
ICI 52
Institutes of Chartered
    Accountants 4, 9ff
Intuition 36ff

Jaguar 124/6
Japan 72/4, 80/1, 123
Jesus 46, 155, 192, 194, 201
Johnson & Johnson 55
Kant, Immanuel 41ff, 65, 163
Kleinwort Benson 88
Kuwaiti Investment Office 52
LBOs 157/9
Levi-Strauss 53
Laing Construction 181/2
LAUTRO 106
Locke, John 22
Luther 31
MacDonalds 55
Machiavelli 31ff, 43, 56, 79
Marks and Spencer 106, 120
Marx, Karl 72
Midland Bank 107
Money laundering 1
Moore, G.E. 23, 36
Motorola 55
National Westminster Bank
    153/5
Nazi Germany 26, 35, 189, 199
N C R 55
Nestle 82, 161
Nissan 79
OPEC 141

Plato 32/3
Quakers 81, 112, 134
Prichard, H. A. 37/8
Refugees 127/8
Religious publishing 77/9
Roman Catholic 179, 193ff
Rothmans 88
Rowntrees 82, 161
Sainsburys 18
Sexual morality 31
Sheppard, Allen 181
Shute, Nevil 94
Socrates 191
South Africa 111, 128ff, 142, 145ff
SSAP s 10/12
Stock Exchange 51, 154, 164
Syllogism 21
Thames Water Authority 171ff
Thatcher, Margaret 137
Third World countries 134ff
Tobacco companies 100, 101
U.S. deficit 198
Utilitarianism 33ff, 44
VISA 101ff
Volvo 71
Wall Street 28
Wittgenstein, L. 23ff.

THE CROSS AND THE SWITCHBLADE

David Wilkerson

One of the best sellers of Christian paperbacks! An amazing and breathtaking description of one man's adventure in faith into New York gangland. If Christianity can work here it will work anywhere.

No Christian should miss this modern Acts of the Apostles. £1.95

JONI

Joni Eareckson Tada

In this international bestseller, Joni, the victim of an accident that left her totally paralysed from the neck down, reveals the struggle to accept and adjust to her handicap.

Joni's story has been made into a full length feature film. £1.95